The Business Zoo

by

Brad James

ISBN: 978-0-692-42807-8

For information address: Brads Tales

jbradfordjames@mac.com

The Business Zoo

Table of Contents

Chapter	**Key Stories**

Acknowledgements

I will begin by thanking my wonderful wife, Tricia, for her patience, suffering and support both during my work years and especially during my time writing this book. She is like having an off line thesaurus and dictionary as I would shout never ending questions about some word, which I would often mispronounce.

My son, Mike, likewise suffered during my early career as it must have seemed to him that I worked endlessly. I was fortunate that Mike did get to share in some of the fun business trips. Now he is a wonderful father himself and I am proud of him every day.

My sister, Sally, has been my biggest fan in life. Our parents, Jake and Dot James, are gone but Sally would agree that from them we both learned to deal with, and even master, the creatures we have confronted in life's zoo.

Our friend, Heidi, who helped me deal with, if not tame, the technology issues of social media such as setting up my blog and then getting all these stories in an acceptable form to publish.

My Mentors and work colleagues, both past, present and gone, you know who you are, and how much you contributed to my learning and growth and to some of the best stories in any book!

Last but never least, a very special thank you goes to Cheryl Jefferson, my writing coach and friend. She knew how to gently prod me into first starting this project and then to coax and encourage me to become a better writer whose work, I hope, she will be proud of. Her husband, the talented Richard Laurent, was able to capture my Zoo concept on the covers.

Preamble

It's a winter night a number of years ago, I am completing a business dinner with one of my European Presidents in his home city. Dinner ends early that evening and he asks if I would like to go back to his home for a drink. He mentions that his wife is there and she always enjoys chatting with me. Sounds great!

His wife, like all our European Presidents' wives or girlfriends was attractive and very smart. She was a social science professor and lectured throughout Europe. We will call her Sylvia. Because her husband had been with my employer, Donn Corporation, for a number of years, Sylvia had met many of our unique people from Donn.

We went to their home and adjourned to the living room for a drink. As soon as we sit, my European President friend seems to disappear from the room and maybe the house.

Our European guys often soared off like eagles. I am left alone with his wife.

Sylvia knew that I was the Chief Financial guy from the U.S. headquarters but she asked me to explain exactly what I did for the Donn group of companies. I covered the normal financial stuff-borrowing money, insurance, taxes and record keeping.

But Sylvia wanted to know more.

I touched on helping the private Donn owners with hiring and sometimes firing managers and setting rewards and incentives. I also explained some of the many crisis matters I had covered which ranged from financial to organizational. I then went into the idea of planning and anticipating outside threats that can damage the Company. I also stated that part of my standard role was to safeguard the Company's assets whether those were hard assets like plants or soft assets like people.

As I was talking, Sylvia listened intently, nodding in understanding, asking for clarification or posing a follow-up question. This went on for an hour until she stopped and smiled. "Brad," she said, "you are really not the head financial person. You are more like the head person in a zoological park. You care for the wild or exotic animals inside. Protect them from each other and the outside world. You help them grow strong. If they behave badly you correct or remove them. At times you even shield them from the owners. And although, it is not your zoo, you would defend it with your life, if need be!"

Over time, I concluded she was right. And ironically, a few years later, I did have to remove her husband from Donn.

Much of my business life was spent dealing with unique creatures, human and animal. To learn to tame your creatures while capturing opportunities, join me in The Business Zoo.

Letter to Readers

Hi, my name is Brad James.

When I "retired" from my first big, public firm, USG Corporation, my staff threw a going away party. They presented me with an unusual gift: a hardbound journal style book with only a Table of Contents. It was actually a list of the titles of stories or tales I had told them on various occasions. They were encouraging me to do what I had often threatened to do-write a book.

Or, more accurately, a business book involving these and other stories I had told. Their Table of Contents/List included almost 50 different titles. Apparently they all thought it was important to document these tales and suggested that I actually write down those stories that had an impact upon them, personally or professionally.

Now I have written them down for you.

My hope is that this book will provide a guide for young people entering or moving up in organizations. Along the way, I try to provide some Rules and Tools to help with critical issues. At the end of each chapter is a summary of the Lessons Learned, for future reference.

Content-wise this is a book about organizations. Private companies, public ones and even not-for-profits; all of which I have worked in and know a bit about. It's a book about how these organizations both function and sometimes dysfunction. It covers most of the key critical areas of management from Selling to Systems; from Boards to Human Resources. The book also covers the major events that impact and change all organizations such as Planning, Mergers and Crisis Management.

Many sections compare and contrast how smaller, private firms and larger, public firms approach and deal with these issues, with a lot of real life stories to help the Reader relate to what these things really mean. I end with the all-encompassing topics of Leadership and Culture that either grow or destroy organizations in a dog-eat-dog way.

To that point, I've been fascinated by animals my whole life. I read about and study them every chance I get. They're remarkably similar to people and sometimes more authentic, honest and true to their nature. That's why I use various animals or creatures to help explain things.

So sit back, take a read and maybe learn something about business and life through The Business Zoo.

1. Ethics and Morality

(It's only Business not Personal)

I Won't Cheat!

That is the official motto of the Little League, whose annual World Series is on TV each August, from Williamsport, PA. The words are on a patch on each uniform. If you've ever watched the LLWS, you might agree that it is far superior to watching most millionaire sports divas play. Recently, Uganda became the first African team to qualify even though most of the boys had only played baseball for two years, usually without shoes until they had to wear them in the tournament! With no family able to afford to come with them, the Uganda team became the favorite of all the other players and fans. That's sportsmanship. You can also sense how much all these kids just love playing the game. True, they are only 10-12, but I really believe most of the Little Leaguers would never cheat. They just want to play ball.

Yet, every year there is a major scandal at the LLWS, about the age of a player, or his home address. Almost all of these scandals can be traced to the kid's parents, coaches or league officials.

So when and how do we go from non-cheating kids to adults with issues on Morality and Ethics?

Black and White Versus Grey

I have been lucky in my business career to have several Mentors. One was George Davis, Chief Financial Officer for the private company, Donn. I was fortunate to both work with and keep in touch with George for years.

George hired me away from the Donn Audit team of Arthur Andersen to report to him in the new position of Corporate Controller. I was in my mid 20's, very eager, and also very idealistic. I was also part of an Arthur Andersen's culture which taught us that clients were not as smart as we were, or they would be advisors like us. I had also advanced rapidly in public accounting so I knew I was smart. But George could see I had a lot to learn.

When I started at Donn, George was old enough to be my recently deceased father. Like my father, George had been in World War II serving as a young bomber pilot and squad leader flying out of Paris and dropping bombs on Germany near the end of the war. His personal life had also been complex with the death of his first wife and raising their adopted son who was in trouble most of the time. After college on the GI Bill, George had worked in public accounting and industry. He joined Donn in his 40s and became the number two person to Donn's founder.

Even though he was busy, somehow George always had time and patience for me. I learned a lot about the people side of business from George, starting with the way he treated me. It was good that George was always patient with me because, in those early years, I tended to question and argue with him about almost everything.

One of our biggest disagreements involved changing our European banker, American Express (AMEX). In those days AMEX did full commercial banking not just credit cards. George decided that our four European businesses were now large and successful enough to work with local banks in each country. Working with local banks would lower borrowing costs and provide us greater flexibility. Our local country Presidents really liked the idea as they would gain prestige and have access to the services of these local banks for their personal business. George and I agreed on every aspect of the deal, except one.

George did not want to tell AMEX that we would be ending our relationship until we had all the new individual country bank lines in place and could switch 100%. I argued that we had such a great, long standing relationship with AMEX that we should give them proper notice regarding our plan. George said we had the most leverage with the new banks while they thought we still had AMEX as an option. He also said AMEX could make our last days miserable by changing our banking terms and conditions. I saw this as very black and white and argued that his approach was morally not correct! George saw a practical solution. We did it his way.

Our European businesses grew with their local banks and within a few years, AMEX had exited commercial banking.

A decade later, George, now in his 60's, starts to retire from Donn. The owner, Don Brown, devised a unique plan where

George goes from five days a week to four days the next year to three days the next year, all with full pay. This provided the company, George and Mr. Brown with a smooth transition. It also kept a trusted resource available if he was needed and a type of insurance policy on the new guy, me! By the time George got down to two days a week, it took me the first day to catch him up. George decided the plan no longer worked and he fully retired.

Nowadays with email it might have been easier to keep someone in the loop but often the really important items were the people issues, which are still not automated, and are best dealt with face-to-face.

Somewhere toward the end of George's extended retirement we went alone to one of our many private lunches. The pattern, at this point in our relationship, was that I spent much of our time updating George on any important business or financial issues and he would offer comments or suggestions if he had any. We had gotten to the point where his input was very limited so often this was more of a courtesy update on my part, just in case George was asked a question by Don Brown.

Now this particular lunch was late in the calendar year. We were almost done with our meal and I had covered all the normal, important items. I was searching my brain for something else to discuss that George might find intellectually interesting or useful even if it wasn't critical to the business. Because Donn was a private company, tax items often fit into this category.

I told George that because the Company was having an unusually profitable year, I had had a meeting with our outside

CPA firm to discuss corporate income taxes. Private firms like Donn always want to minimize taxes. They had suggested a potential income tax deferral strategy that other clients were considering. Under the then existing tax code we could report a tax loss in this year offset with a tax gain the next year. While this strategy wouldn't save us taxes, it would defer the payment of taxes for a year or more. I went on to say that our outside CPA firm was also advising that this could help individuals as well. Knowing that George had occasionally used personal income tax strategies, like oil and gas partnerships, he might want to talk to them about his own situation.

George almost spilled his coffee as he put his cup down hard and loudly said "You can't do that!"

I thought maybe he had misunderstood what I said so I reiterated that our outside CPA firm was recommending this new tax strategy to us and to other clients.

George, uncharacteristically, is now almost shouting, "You can't do that!" and this time he adds, "It's illegal!"

I assured him that it was not illegal as our CPA tax experts would actually help to package this and make some money by charging us along the way.

George then gave me the ultimate, unexpected, response, "It's immoral because you are cheating the U.S. Government!"

At that point I remembered some urgent, nonexistent meeting or phone call, so we had to wrap up our lunch. As it was the end of George's two days in the office, I thought this matter would soon be forgotten and I alone could decide whether the Company would pursue this tax strategy or not.

A couple days later, my Administrative Assistant, Kathy, comes into my office. As a longtime trusted employee of Donn, she often took care of all kinds of critical and sensitive matters, initially for George and now for me. Kathy knew everything that was going on and would handle all kinds of calls and office business without needing to get us involved.

This time she comes to my door with a puzzled look. She asks me if the company's federal income tax audit we had worked on for over a year was over. I said yes, we had agreed on all open points and the agent, who I will call Joe, was just finalizing his report. This did not help Kathy's look but she said that Joe, our internal revenue agent, was on the phone and had a question for me. I told her it was probably just some detail one of his bosses asked about and I would take the call. I would then have her help me get him whatever he needed so we could wrap-up our federal income tax audit.

After Joe and I exchanged pleasantries, he said this call was not about our recent federal income tax audit which was concluding just as we had agreed. Rather, Joe said, it had come to his attention, from an unnamed caller, that Donn was considering a questionable tax strategy on the advice of their outside CPA firm. Joe wanted me to tell him exactly who at our CPA firm was proposing this. He also wanted me to tell him the names of the CPA firm's other clients who had been encouraged to try this questionable tax strategy!

George, my old boss, friend and mentor, had turned me and his beloved Company into the IRS!

As the songwriter Harry Chapin might have said in his classic "Taxi," "Another man might have been angry, another man might have been hurt..." I suppose I was both at that moment. But I often lecture young people that when you are asked a very hard question, you should take a breath and say something or you will lose the battle. I told Joe that the Company had not yet adopted this tax strategy, let alone included it on a federal tax return. Therefore, I did not have to discuss this or anything about it with him at this time. Then I nicely said goodbye and thanked him for his interest. Joe never called back on that one.

George and I still met twice a week until he fully retired. The next time we were alone, at lunch, outside the office, I told him of my surprising call from the IRS agent, Joe. George smugly said he had called Joe because he really did not want me to proceed. The smug, almost defiant, look reminded me of how I must have appeared to George when over the years I occasionally won an argument.

I continued to have lunches with George for the next twenty-five years, long after Donn Corporation was sold and I had moved to Chicago. I saw him in his last days of hospice care before he died several years ago. I miss him. He was more than a mentor; he was my life-long trusted advisor and close friend.

I regularly thought of George and his wise advice over the rest of my own career as a chief financial officer, especially one day in the early 1990's. It was during USG Corporation's first financial restructuring. USG owed about $1 billion to 70 banks in a syndicate. As our sales had fallen and our earnings had become losses, we were about to default on the interest payments to this bank group. These same banks also handled all of our cash management, payroll, and payments to critical trade vendors. USG's Treasurer had quietly arranged a whole new set of banks to whom we would turn over these activities, the night before we defaulted on our first bank syndicate. We did that with no formal notice to our current bank group because they could seize all our cash in the accounts to offset the interest even if it meant payroll and vendor checks would bounce. I felt bad; we did it anyhow. George certainly would have understood.

Jessica, a young woman I mentor, told me recently that it is important to try to remember as many decisions your mentor made and told you about, since later you may be faced with the same issue yourself.

Because sometimes the world of business and life is black and white but often it is grey.

Wizards and Grease

Much of the world and especially the worlds of politics and business run on Grease; in fact, Grease is its main fuel. Here we use Grease as a verb meaning "to lubricate or smear" - not a rusty hinge but rather the palm of a hand with coin.

I probably ran into Grease much earlier in my business life than I recall. Often when one is young and idealistic, you assume everyone else is the same. But in the financial restructuring of my company, USG Corporation, Grease had a lasting impact. Now you might think that when a former Fortune 500 company can no longer pay its interest or principle on $3 billion of bank and bond debt that something as financially and morally costly as Grease would never show up; but somehow it always does. More trouble, more Grease.

Grease can probably be traced back centuries to when some King got in trouble, involving a woman, gambling or money, same as nowadays. It had to be big trouble or the King could just deal with it himself. But what if he needed help, and fast?

The King would ask his grand Wizard (read lawyer or banker) and the Wizard would request some unrelated personal payment or benefit to pull the King out of trouble. Each time the King got in trouble after that, and depending how bad the trouble was, the requests by the Wizard got more and more outrageous.

If the Wizard was really bold he might even make a deal with the King's enemy (like his son or a neighboring King) while still serving his current King. A really grand Wizard could ride this horse for years through different Kings, Popes etc. In those days there were no rules on conflicts of interest or SEC disclosure requirements. But as good as ancient Wizards were, they would be considered rank amateurs by today's standards.

When individuals cannot pay their debts, their lenders just repossess the car, or with more difficultly, these days, the house. With a large corporation, like USG, with thousands of employees and over 200 plants, it's harder. It's even more complicated when the big company like USG owes 70 banks and a half dozen different bond issues with different claims and over 10,000 bondholders. That's along with your normal trade vendors, special litigation claimants like asbestos and lastly, of course, your poor shareholders. It is therefore much harder for one category of debtor to just repo your auto to settle your debt. So to solve this complex situation, the various creditor groups form Committees.

The concept of Committees seems fair and a practical way to approach a complex problem. Because a big company like USG owes money to so many different types of creditors who all want to protect their own unique position or rights, you cannot just have one large committee. Instead, you have several separate Committees which are comprised of representatives of the debt holders and Wizards in the form of lawyers, accountants and investment bankers. This allows each Committee to study the issues from their own perspective and then negotiate in their group's best interests. The process sounds logical even though the Company must eventually get all the Committees to agree on all the same things at the same time. Believe it or not, this complex process can work well until the Grease shows up.

Shortly after Wizards are picked by each Committee, they start to act as if everything is about them rather than trying to solve the financial crisis. They assume an all-knowing attitude about everything and many revert to Tom Wolfe's aptly termed "masters of the universe" status. They have all been taught, in their particular firm's Wizard classes, that they are certainly superior not only to the other Wizards working for other Committees but certainly superior to those Company people, who again, are in default. Reinforcing this attitude is the fact that, as a group, the Wizards are truly Masters at the use of Grease against those poor struggling companies in default.

USG had a Bank Committee and two major Bondholder Committees. Each Committee had at least two Wizard groups working with them. Every month USG gets a large invoice from all these outside Wizards plus its own Company hired Wizards. You see, we have to hire our own legal and financial Wizards to help us work with all the Committee Wizards. After paying these bills for many months we start to realize some of the harsh realities of the Restructuring process.

To understand the specific details of our Company, each Committee's Wizards needs to review tons of information about us. Some things are easy to deal with - all of our loan/debt agreements, our financial projections, lists of our major properties and legal and tax structure. Some things are more complicated like our asbestos history, environmental history and active litigation. This all involves numerous boxes of data.

USG needs to give this same information to all the Committees and, to all their Accountants, Lawyers or Bankers.

So one of our bright young staff, Mary, devises a color coded labeling and index system for what seems like truckloads of boxes we are shipping each week to the New York based Wizards, especially to their law firms. After which, we would have the pleasure of receiving another large bill for them to review the information and talk to their Committees. Sometimes, on very complex stuff such as litigation, one or more of the law firms might ask for everything to be sent a second time. Was this to avoid excess Xerox or copying machine hours at their office or because so many of their people were just so excited to see these documents (and bill us) that they could not keep up with the in-house demand? We only knew that after we sent the boxes we were always billed for a review. These were, after all, quality, famous NYC firms just doing their jobs for their Committees. We, those at fault, would never question whether or how often the work was actually done. At least until one day...

On our weekly NYC trips, we always tried to visit the offices of at least one of the Committee people or their advisors. We did this to be friendly and inclusive and to see where everyone worked so we had some frame of reference on our endless conference calls. Basically, we were trying to build relationships with everyone, even our adversaries. So this one day, months into the process, I and a couple of my team members show up, for the first time, at the head office of one of the Committee's Wizards. We were escorted into the senior person's private office to wait for their team. In the corner piled neatly and high were two sets of our USG color-coded, labeled, numbered and indexed boxes. Unopened. We had, of course, already been billed, twice for their review. Can you say, Grease?

A few months later in our multi-year financial Restructuring process we had been making very little progress on fixing our debt structure. We were going to New York City weekly, meeting with any Committee or their advisors we could find but with no real progress. Then one day on a Thursday, the head Wizard of one of the Committee's advisors urgently calls my office. The head Wizard has a brainstorm idea that can move the whole process, if not the world, forward. We are all ears. But the head Wizard will only explain this great idea to me, the Company's CFO, alone, over a dinner the next night in Chicago at a new restaurant we had discussed during one of our many idle moments in New York City.

Our team, and especially our equivalent company Wizards, were very skeptical and concerned about this, as they said, unheard-of-approach. I responded by saying since we were getting nowhere in our Restructuring process other than a lot of meetings, phone calls and paying Wizard's bills why not spend or waste an evening checking it out. Besides, this Wizard was willing to come to Chicago versus requesting that I fly to New York! The dinner meeting was on.

The head Wizard and I had a three and a half hour dinner at the new Chicago restaurant. We ate and drank everything on their extensive menu. We talked about many things: families, backgrounds, business and even USG and its issues. There was nothing new, no breakthrough idea until the end. As we wound up a very long evening, the Wizard explained. You see, the next day it was critical for the Wizard to be in Chicago for an important non-business event. I then realized that USG had paid for the first class round-trip flight, the very nice hotel suite and probably a small breakfast after this huge dinner. Grease.

The only fun experience we had with Grease occurred about halfway through our three-year process. We were, again, at a total dead-end with all the Committees and their Wizards. We were throwing out ideas and no one was catching them. We would have lunch and dinner meetings and sometimes people came just to eat the food (New York deal food is tremendous). We made offers to go to the best new NYC restaurants and only the most junior people from the Committees would show and leave our dinner early to work on some other, apparently more important or pressing deal. This went on for what seemed like months. One day with our Company team and our own Wizards, who had to show, I came up with an idea to jumpstart this seemingly endless process.

It was near the end of the month and the time that we paid our own and all the Committees' Wizards' fees and expense bills. These were now costing USG millions a month. As CFO, I said that the Company was not going to pay any Advisor's bills, including our own this month or any other month until we actually made, in our eyes, some real progress on trying to restructure our debts.

Our own Wizards almost had heart attacks and said we could not do that, all Advisors had to be paid! I said we had paid everyone for a year or more to date and had nothing to show for it. Furthermore, what exactly were the Advisors going to do? Sue the Company? We were already in Default of all this debt! Or would three different Advisors file for Involuntary Bankruptcy of USG and perhaps ruin their Committees' chances of getting any money ever! The way we were going, the Company would eventually run out of all its cash and unless we got some action on fixing our debt problems, we could end up in a full liquidation that benefitted no one!

We called the Committees, they told their Wizards, there were frantic phone calls, much bad language, and, within a week we had a series of meetings with the Committees and their Advisors and made some modest but decent progress. Then we paid the bills. The process of Restructuring seemed to move a lot better from then on. Grease. But useful Grease this time.

Sometimes people ask me: Did we ever confront those cheating Wizards or threaten to report them? No, we did not. What we did do is remember the episodes and sometime, at some point in the three year deal we privately made a veiled comment to the offender to let them know that we knew.

Which leads us to our final story in this Chapter.

It's Only Business (or Hell's Kitchen Revisited)!

Early in the financial restructuring of USG Corporation, I first heard the phrase, It's Only Business. It could have come from one of our own Restructuring lawyers or bankers. Regardless, it seemed to me, that the phrase must have originated in New York City. Often the line was used when I, or one of my Company's restructuring team, was especially upset with some of the daily bad behavior we were subjected to at the hands of one of our Creditor Committees or their Wizard advisors.

For example, when a creditor advisor went back on a hard fought agreement that we had already explained to another creditor group, one of our own advisors would say, It's Only Business. When someone outright lied to our face or on a conference call, our experts would say, It's Only Business. When we would get so upset with all the nasty deal making tactics or the constant use of

Grease and say terrible things directly to one of the creditor advisors, they would say relax, It's Only Business.

Early on I asked one of our USG head Investment Wizards, who'd spent most of his life in New York City, exactly what this phrase meant? And why was it that those who understood the meaning would never get as upset with each other as I got?

My Wizard, Michael, explained that the phrase went back to "the old neighborhood." The idea was that there were things in life that were "Business" and things in life that were "Personal." He went on to say that in "the old neighborhood" the Business problems became Personal when someone would find you in an alley and smash in the back of your head with a baseball bat. He said this rather matter-of-factly. Since Michael was my investment banker, not one of the Creditor Committees, I felt I could ask him at least one follow-up question without becoming Personal so I asked where, exactly, was "the old neighborhood" people referred to. He looked at my Ohio born naiveté and, with a worldly smile, said it was Hell's Kitchen, of course.

The Hell's Kitchen he was referring to was not the television reality show starring a famous London chef who seemed capable of hitting contestants with a variety of pots and pans. Rather, my investment banker friend was referring to a part of Manhattan that became famous or infamous in the late 1800's and early 1900's, as the home of immigrants from many different countries, starting with the Irish, then the Italians and later the Hispanics. The area became famous for its violence in real life, in literature, and in the movies. Vito Corleone's family in The Godfather and the various gangs in West Side Story, were all attributed to Hell's Kitchen.

What I found fascinating was that my banker friend, Michael, and most of our deal's lawyers and bankers were not of Irish or Italian background. In addition, they all lived on the Upper East Side or in trendy Brooklyn Heights. Likewise, the historic Hell's Kitchen area had become rather successful and well to do over the past forty years.

The area is still home to places like the famous Actor's Studio and many well-known personalities have lived there. Some, like James Cagney or Mickey Rourke, I could envision using a blunt object versus others like Tom Hanks.

So I still was not sure about this phrase and the baseball bat analogy. After more research, and more frustrating personal experiences, I created my own definition for It's Only Business.

Now my definition was more simple and straightforward, even if it was not morally pleasing to everyone. I came to believe that It's Only Business meant there were two standards or codes of behavior. One code for Business and one for your Personal life.

In Business, you could lie to people (or more politely, not tell anything like the whole truth), take massive liberties with the technical definitions of corporate or security laws (be that conflict of interests, improper trading, ignoring confidentiality agreements, etc.) receive Grease payments with no justification or factual basis, etc. You could do this five or six working days a week and it was okay since it was "Only Business." At night, on the weekends or even during the week with close friends and family your

"Personal" code of behavior was beyond reproach and you would never do anything like the Business actions.

Thus, many of the characters we came in contact with in our three years of financial restructuring had no problem reconciling these two standards of behavior in their own minds or that of their business associates. After all they never resorted to hitting us with a baseball bat or any other blunt instrument. They just hit us with large fees!

I am sure many people found this dual code comforting. My problem was that my Italian mother had always taught me a different view of the world. To Dot James, the way you acted in school, at work, in sports or at home was a reflection of how you were raised. It was critical to her that you be consistent in your values and behavior, in your approach to others and the world. Although I never had a chance to ask her about this dual philosophy I had been subjected to, I knew what her view would have been. As a second generation Italian from a rough part of South Philly I am sure she would have understood the baseball bat part better than I ever did. And as one of the first women to enlist in the WACs during WWII she would have had strong and definite views on the timing and use of force as well.

But my mother would have really enjoyed one of the last times I heard the phrase about Business and Personal.

After the USG restructuring I moved from CFO to running parts of the Company's operations. A few years later, as USG was going through its twentieth or so Reorganization, USG's new Chairman, Bill, and I, mutually decided I would retire to "pursue other interests" as the saying goes. I had known Bill my whole tenure at USG and we had been peers and friends for years.

As we spent our last business afternoon alone together discussing my retirement he paid me a great compliment. Bill commented that I was like almost no one else he had ever met in business. I asked what he meant. He explained that, in the decade he had known me, I acted the same in my "Personal" dealings with people as I acted in my "Business" dealings. By contrast most individuals Bill knew acted differently in those two worlds.

I smiled, realizing I had never learned the lesson of:

It's Only Business! And I was really glad I hadn't!

Lessons Learned from Ethics and Morality

The slogan, I Won't Cheat! should be used not just by the Little League, but everyone in life and business.

When you are young and idealistic, choices seem black or white. When you are older or in charge, choices seem more grey.

The more trouble in business, politics or life, the more needs or uses there are for "helpful" Wizards and their Grease.

You can sometimes get things done by withholding Grease.

In our ever changing, complex world is it possible to approach life and business with the same rules? YES!

Can our work or the crisis we encounter cause us to compromise or change our moral compass?
> Sadly, Yes.

Hell's Kitchen is not so bad these days; blame something else!

2. Management Fraud
(And Other Bad Behavior)

Introduction to Fraud

Fraud, like Grease and many other topics we cover, goes back to the beginning of people and time. The most accepted definition of Fraud is an intent to deceive, to inflict a loss on others while receiving a gain for yourself. Fraud occurs in every culture and every type of organization-charities, government and, of course, business. It can range from common issues like improper tax deductions to the headline stories about billion dollar Ponzi schemes.

Our focus here, however, will be on business firms where it occurs from bookkeepers to the Board of Directors. That said, we will concentrate primarily on those people who should know better, people who already make excellent money and who often believe they never did anything wrong. Management Fraud.

Accountants and Management Fraud

Accountants/CPAs have spent a lot of time thinking about Fraud. As a result, the profession has always stressed the need for strong internal controls. These range from simple steps like physical control or access (cash registers and system passwords) to administrative measures like job descriptions and segregation of duties (depositing daily cash vs. posting receivable ledger) to procedural steps like reviewing and analyzing accounts. The next level of internal control is supervision, which, you will learn from the stories that follow, is usually where the problem occurs. Good supervision involves actually understanding and reviewing or approving what your staff does. Then all this needs to be audited either internally or externally, which means fees for the CPA firms who set up the rules in the first place.

What has developed is the concept that the outside Auditors/CPA's job is not to detect Fraud but to report on the financial statements as a whole. Many Frauds are small in dollars and therefore, are in the words of accountants, immaterial.

I would prefer that auditors took a more proactive approach.

My personal experience in Management Fraud, at both private and publicly audited companies, is that the outside Auditors/CPAs are useless when it comes to detecting or notifying people of a possible Fraud. I have had Senior Audit partners in several countries apologize for their firm when major frauds occurred.

Bottom line-do not expect much outside help. Dealing with Management Fraud is primarily an internal, difficult and time-consuming activity. It is also an activity that is best performed by one person or a small group of people who can work quietly and with access to the very top of the organization.

Sometimes a company can accidentally contribute to a Fraud.

Corporate Culture and Management Fraud

Corporate culture is also a huge factor in Management Fraud. This can vary vastly by company, size and whether they are private or public firms. A theme that reoccurs in both big and small organizations is the pressure to meet goals. The accounting profession found that this was the case in up to 80% of the instances of corporate fraud. You see, bonus plans are based on hitting certain targets for sales or earnings. All of this pressure to meet goals relates to the earlier definition of Fraud which is to seek personal gain.

Smaller private firms, such as my former employer Donn Corp., usually don't have elaborate procedures and systems. They also do not have a large corporate staff to oversee or review things as part of their regular duties. But sometimes the very core of a smaller, private firm's culture can be its biggest weakness.

At Donn, like many entrepreneurial businesses, the core driver was sales growth. The theory was to sell, then eventually you will make money to keep growing. The senior operating and sales people were very well rewarded with above industry level salaries, large cash bonuses, extremely fancy company cars, and lavish, unquestioned expense accounts. As Donn grew larger it became a major problem to watch everything and everybody.

By contrast, public companies like my former employers USG or IMC Global, often tried to avoid these pitfalls with Internal Audit functions, extensive procedures, and codes of business conduct which dealt with conflicts of interest, supplier relationships, compliance with laws, and personal behavior.

But Code cannot dictate or predict people's behavior. Internal Auditors can help but usually after the fact. Often large public companies and their Boards place too much faith or hope in these tools. Some stories of private and public firms may explain why. As an old saying goes, there are a million Fraud stories in the business world, here are but a few!

Management Fraud in Public Companies

To Prosecute or Not

Public firms often do not prosecute cases of proven fraud even if they have Codes that say they do. I know this because I have been involved in a dozen conversations where I was the only one suggesting the Company call the authorities. Now, this does not mean that public firms won't try to get their money back or threaten legal action. The main reason companies cite that they do not prosecute is that it costs time and money. But the real reason large public firms don't take action is that they are afraid. Afraid of having to give depositions; afraid to go to court and mostly afraid the Company will look stupid or mean or bad or worse yet, wrong! So staying with this theme and to avoid hurting anyone's innocent families we will tell real Fraud stories without real names or titles. Certain old work friends can feel free to guess at the true identities.

Grooming a Senior Corporate Executive's Expenses

As individuals rise to the top of the senior corporate ranks, they get many benefits and privileges. But this is not enough for some people. A certain Senior Corporate Executive needed more. So the Executive started charging personal expenses like hair stylists and the cost of a holiday staff party. The total was very minor compared to the Executive's salary.

But here are a couple little understood facts. Expense reports for senior executives are reviewed and approved internally by other senior executives! Now some senior people actually perform this review as though it is important; others not. But what should be common knowledge is that Internal Audit will spot check all senior executives' expense reports.

Our Senior Executive's improper grooming and party expenses turned a spot check into a multi-year full blown review of all expense reports and departmental spending. The Senior Corporate Executive abruptly left the company "to pursue other interests." This dreaded corporate jargon phrase usually means they were fired or reached some impasse with their boss.

Perhaps they learned a lesson and went straight with their next employer! But somehow I doubt it. You see there are serial defrauders in this world like there are serial everything else.

The Downfall of a Corporate Department Czar

Many large public company headquarters are full of Corporate Departments that are run like fiefdoms controlled by czars. These Czars take on huge, undeserved power because their Bosses let them. The Bosses let this occur either because the area is too technical (taxes, environmental), too legal (legal, corporate secretary, or labor law), or too boring or detailed (insurance, real estate, payroll), for the Boss to either understand or to influence the Boss' next promotion. Even Internal Audit finds these areas difficult to deal with.

This particular Corporate Department Czar-we will abbreviate as Czar-decided to divorce his wife to pursue other younger interests. This wife called the corporate headquarters.

She reported a kickback scheme the Czar had been using. On projects involving outside consultants, the Czar mainly hired a close friend's firm to do the work. When the friend's firm was paid, they made out a separate check to the Czar or a shell firm he controlled.

The Czar's wife even brought into the corporate headquarters indisputable proof and details that showed how the fraud worked and the relative magnitude of it!

The Corporation and the Senior Bosses were shocked. The Czar left the company.

After the financial settlements he made with his former employer and then his wife, who took most of what was left, he had less money to pursue anything or anyone else.

It's the old moral that Hell or even Czars hath no fury like a woman scorned!

Management Fraud in a Private Company

The Verdict: I am sitting in a courtroom and the Judge is announcing the following verdict:

Multiple counts of embezzlement, guilty!

Multiple counts of theft and grand theft, guilty!

Multiple counts of false pretenses/conspiracy, guilty!

Multiple counts of abuse of position/fraud, guilty!

Multiple counts of false accounting/records, guilty!

Multiple counts of tax evasion/fraud, guilty!

On all 52 crimes, guilty!

The prison time for this many felonies will be decades!

I am not the accused; but my company, Donn, the local police criminal fraud unit, and I are the accusers.

The accused is a former friend and colleague who we will name ED, for European Defalcator. ED is not in Court with me.

Two weeks before the trial began, he convinced a different judge that he needed his passport so that he could research a new business located in a neighboring country. He left the country he was born in; the country he had worked in all his life; the country where his family and friends lived. He ended up in another nearby European country that did not have an extradition treaty. But let's go back in time to how all this happened.

Donn's European Presidents

Donn's private company focus was on growth in sales, then in profits. Donn offered large base salaries, large bonus opportunities and titles like President. But mostly what Donn offered was freedom. Freedom from large company headquarters staff. Freedom from written codes of conduct. Freedom to develop the local markets your way, as long as you were successful.

In each European country Donn entered, success quickly followed. As construction and buildings grew so did the local Donn business. With this success, the local European Presidents were treated like Kings. Kings appointed by Donn owners with ever increasing financial rewards. Donn's local Presidents had the best company cars available, Bentleys and Mercedes, and unlimited expense accounts for travel and entertainment. They were also Kings in their geographic area both with local suppliers and business and civic leaders.

In private companies, the line between business and personal actions and expenses often blurs. Let's see how this line became very blurry for one of Donn's European Presidents, ED. And remember, all of these activities actually occurred.

The Crimes of Donn's European Defalcator, ED

The Travel Agency: The local travel agency books all of ED's and his Donn company's travel; this becomes a huge part of their business. ED starts asking for small favors, like making some of his trips look like visits to cities with major customers instead of seaside resorts with young lady guests.

Charter Services and Diamonds: A local pilot would be paid to fly ED to visit large customers or to other Donn European locations. But no actual business trips occurred. When the pilot was in Amsterdam, he would pick up some nice diamond necklace or bracelet and deliver this merchandise to ED. The final delivery point was, of course, one of ED's special lady friends.

The Used Car Business: A luxury car was acquired by ED in a large major city and driven back to the Donn operation. It was then taken to the local car dealer who legitimately supplied the Donn managers with company cars. The car dealer was instructed to buy the car, at a substantial discount, so he could resell it and give ED cash for the "fair" trade-in value of about $20,000. The car dealer later told me he still lost money on this deal. Apparently that day ED really needed some quick cash!

Horsing around with Construction Kickbacks: The local Donn plant was growing and needed to expand. An area builder was hired to do the work with no other competitive bids. ED knew the builder because they both owned a racehorse together or rather Donn owned half the horse. For each stage of the construction he would present ED with two bills: one for the real amount of the work and one that was marked up 10% to be paid by the Donn company. The difference was a kickback, by the builder to his friend ED. Over the course of the project that amounted to some $200,000 today.

Being a Good Sport in the Community: ED joined a group of local businessmen who helped keep the local professional sports team in their area by investing in the team. ED did not invest in the team, Donn's money did. We sold this ownership, at a large discount, but had we kept it, today it could have paid for a lot of ED's crimes. Sports teams everywhere are hot, hot, hot! So let's look at how you detect and deal with Management Fraud.

Detecting High Level Management Fraud

Sometimes the external auditors can help with their memos on Internal Control. These documents are written at the end of an audit and should be reviewed face-to-face with the auditors by someone outside the local operation. In the case of Donn, these memos regularly pointed out the lack of adequate expense documentation and controls at our European locations.

Ultimately, the only real way to detect this type of high level fraud is with the help of another local manager. After all, Fraud can rarely remain totally hidden. Fraud also needs helpers, and somewhere in the local business, at least one other manager knows. But knowing and telling are two different things.

So the real key to detecting this type of Fraud is to build strong relationships between the company's owners or someone at the headquarters and some of the local managers other than the local

President. Remember, it takes time to build trust and this will require a number of visits and private dinners. Even so, someone at the local operation must be upset enough and trust you enough to tell you about the Fraud. They then need to help you gather proof. This is a very difficult thing to do. The local President is their Boss and maybe even their friend. If word gets out, or if they are wrong, they will be fired, period.

In addition to local help, you need legal advice because the definition of a crime varies from country to country. Also, while white-collar crime may seem very criminal to a company's owners or their representatives, the local authorities may not view it so drastically. Strong local legal advice can help you understand all this and how you should pursue it.

Making your Fraud Case

Before you get your bosses or owners all upset and before you confront your defrauder, you must make sure you are right and that you are dealing with a provable case of high level fraud. You cannot accuse someone of such a crime of trust and fiduciary duty unless you are absolutely right. What does this mean? It means you cannot go on hearsay, even from one of the other local managers who claims to know; it could be a case of an overly ambitious or upset subordinate stretching the truth. It means you cannot rely on one or two possibly explainable events; you need multiple examples of fraud. You must also get to the original source documents like the duplicate construction invoices. If you are wrong in accusing a senior, well-respected executive, you will be fired, not them! And you should be fired because you did not do enough work.

Making sure that I had done all this work and had a provable case of Fraud is probably one of the most difficult and soul-searching things I have ever done. Donn's local Presidents were like Kings; to confront and take down a King, you must be right!

Confronting and Containing the Accused

To return to our story, you are now ready to confront ED with your facts. You owe it to ED even though you know you are right. It is best to meet ED with your Boss or Owner, and probably with legal counsel. It is also best to meet ED outside the local office and without ED knowing what is going on. And while you are having this meeting, it is best to have someone else at the local company headquarters changing all the entry locks to the building and to ED's office. This ensures that no further evidence will be removed. Now this may sound cold or like overkill but believe me, it is for the best. Do not doubt that ED would do or say anything to get out of this mess!

How and where did we meet and confront ED? Through the travel agency invoices, of course! We knew that ED had booked a phony business trip with a lady friend to attend a charity ball. We booked a suite at the hotel where he was staying. Donn's owner called ED on the phone said he was in town and needed to see him. ED came to our suite. He was shocked to see the Owner, his direct European boss, the financial guy/me, and a guy who looked like and was a lawyer. He was more shocked when we explained why we were there and started to show him evidence.

We then asked ED if he had any explanation for what we were showing him or what he had done. He asked who had provided us with this information; we said that was not important. His main response was that we did not understand. That he had spent the money on the Donn business. That in our construction industry, he had to spend a lot of money buying women to entertain our customers (as an accountant I sat there trying to calculate how many entertaining women it would take for all the missing money.) He talked a lot but he said nothing. There really was no explanation other than the one he could not bring himself to say, that he stole from the Company. Stole from the Company that was paying him a huge salary and bonus. The Company that let him drive any car he wanted or travel on business anywhere he thought he needed to. He just stole. He had committed high level Management Fraud and somehow he got caught.

I then explained the next steps to ED. We had prepared a formal resignation from his position as President and we wanted him to sign it now or we would fire him regardless.

I asked to meet with ED in a couple days at his former office. The office and all of our facilities were now off limits. He would drop off the expensive Company car, all his Company credit cards and any other Company property. We would go through his office and let him remove personal items. Most importantly, if he had any better explanation as to why this had occurred he could explain it then, as the following week, we were turning our information over to the local police. We were also filing criminal and civil charges and suing to recover the missing funds. He asked if we could avoid the criminal charges. Only, we repeated, if he could explain all this away. He signed the resignation form and quietly left.

ED left the meeting upset but without any sign of remorse or shame. I was very upset with ED. Upset that he stole from us. Upset that I had spent agonizing months investigating his fraud. And maybe the most upset that he had nothing to say.

The Company Transition and the Aftermath

The next day all of us were at the local Donn office. We had called ED's direct reports at home and asked them to arrive early for a meeting. The meeting included the local office staff and plant managers. We explained briefly what had occurred and that ED had resigned. We explained the temporary, transitional management structure. We tried to balance the cold truth with a sense of going forward. Some told us of their limited knowledge or innocent involvement in what had occurred.

Over the next few days we dealt with a public announcement and calls to major customers and vendors. When we went through ED's office and files, the case just got worse. And then a very strange thing happened. Outside people showed up to explain and apologize before we even called them! The owner of the travel agency. The pilot with the Amsterdam diamond connection. This made things even worse for ED. The construction/horse owning buddy, we actually had to call in. I met with ED for the last time. He offered no explanations. He asked again if we could avoid criminal charges. No.

Dealing with the Police

Our local lawyers had set up a meeting with the local police fraud unit. We were near their regional headquarters for this type of crime. We met with a Senior Detective who explained their rules. Once we filed criminal charges, we cannot retract. It's their Case now. Once we turn over all of our evidence we are out of the investigation. It's their Case now. If the investigation implicates any of our other managers, only they decide whether to charge them. Once any trial starts we will show up to testify or we will be held in contempt and arrested the next time we land in their country.

We were briefed by our lawyers on all this beforehand. But this is a major reason that large, public companies avoid criminal charges in the case of employee fraud; you are no longer in control of the process once you start it.

My new friend, the Senior Detective, was in control. Over the next few months before the trial, he interviewed dozens of company vendors and employees and a number of ED's lady friends. The lady friends ranged from an employee's daughter to a local beauty contest winner. But their stories often suggested that they were more arm candy companions than anything else.

The stories and the crimes kept piling up. It was not looking good for old ED. You see, people who were uncertain about talking to a young U.S. financial guy always talked to the local Senior Detective! In retrospect, the Senior Detective probably did too good of a job. ED must have heard from a number of people that they were willingly confessing. And this may be why he flew the coop two weeks before his trial and conviction. But some common threads came together.

Common Underlying Themes to the Fraud

The main theme behind this and many Management Frauds is ego. Personal, inflated, fueled by initial success, ego. It became important to ED that he look important. Important to the local community, the sports team, the horse, the lady friends.

This ego issue, ties into something that may be unique to smaller, private companies: The line between the business and the personal becomes totally blurred.

The local Travel Agency, the Car Dealer and others told the police and me that ED had assured them that he was an owner of the local company and that this was just to avoid taxes.

But there was a more vicious theme or two as well. When initially questioned by any of his staff on an item, ED would state that the Donn owners and headquarters people knew all about what he and others were doing. This line of attack creates a real problem for even the most loyal or honest of employees: who can they trust and tell about this? The other wrongful thing ED did was to involve some of his staff with gifts, tickets to events and personal trips like a silent bribe, paid by Donn.

Donn's Response to ED's Actions

After this, we tried to address the problem head-on with all our International managers. We held a big meeting with all the local Presidents (ED could not come, he was in exile) and their senior financial people. Donn's owner and I explained in a lot of detail what had occurred and the consequences to ED. We also made it clear that this type of bad behavior would not be tolerated. We also said that if anyone had anything to tell us, do it now, not when we might stumble across it. Everyone agreed, nodded their heads and pledged their undying loyalty and trust.

A year later, my financial guy, Dale, and I discovered the same type of Fraud at another location by another local President I will call ED2. A number of the Fraud items were similar but ED2 had his own style:

Six Company cars in his name or his family.

ED2 loved real estate - he had our Company buy him an apartment and a warehouse!

Again ED2 was very highly paid. His fraud may only have been worth a quarter to half million in today's dollars; but maybe he started late!

The local police heard our story but chose not to pursue criminal charges since white-collar crimes were not popular at that time!

Lessons Learned from Management Fraud

Codes of Conduct and Internal Audit rarely catch Fraud.

What can catch Fraud are strong and wide relationships between local managers and someone at the headquarters.

Too much power and control whether in a corporate department czar or Presidents who are far from headquarters can be bad.

People need to be actively managed and their expenses reviewed.

For most Senior Executive Fraud, criminal actions should be pursued in spite of the risks and lack of control.

Personal ego is a critical trait that drives success, but unchecked or inflated egos can lead to Fraud.

Often, a Company's own culture or reward system fosters this type of bad behavior.

Management Fraud destroys trust, friendship and careers as well as marriages and families. Is it worth it?

3. Crisis Management
(Manage it and Survive)

Introduction to a Crisis

Most crises, in life and business, involve money. Or the lack of it, or the high cost of it, and on and on. Even organizational or technology crises often get back to money.

Every day in the business news we have some company in any variety of industries getting itself into a crisis. It does not matter the specific industry, or company size; one day, all businesses and other organizations have a crisis usually involving money. In fact, most money or financial crises then lead to organizational or business downsizing crises.

Here we will focus on two business crises. One at the small, privately owned Donn, and one at the large, public USG. Both were manufacturing companies in the cyclical construction industry, which played a supporting role in both situations.

As we examine, compare, and contrast these situations we will look at how to manage and survive a Crisis and offer some Rules and Tools to help get you and your organization through one, with your mental health and some of your assets, intact.

The Donn Crisis

Donn Corporation produced metal ceiling systems and was growing rapidly. By the mid-1970s, sales and income had doubled every five years. Donn's domestic plants were running full out. The only immediate problem was that Donn's main raw material, steel, was getting harder to buy and more expensive. These higher steel costs were being passed onto customers.

Donn just needed more steel, period!

To solve this problem, Donn purchased a year's supply at a fixed price from a steel warehouse. It would stretch Donn's bank line of credit but the products would sell out fast and at a high profit. Don Brown, the owner, knew he might be risking the whole company, but this was the kind of bold move that only a small, entrepreneurial organization could pull off!

Then, as quickly as the steel shortage began, it ended. Suddenly there was all the steel you needed at half the price. Simultaneously, a construction downturn occurred and, production levels fell by half. Donn had a year's worth of steel with their bank lines of credit maxed out. A major financial crisis.

Adding fuel to the fire, Donn's long time chief financial officer, George Davis was at the Cleveland Clinic, having heart bypass surgery, adding a major organizational crisis to the major financial crisis.

The result: a perfect storm of crises.

Approach to the Donn Crisis

First, Face Reality:

When any person or organization faces a life-threatening event, there are some initial steps that must be made. First, everyone needs to face reality and be on the same page. At a smaller, private firm that can be easier and faster to achieve than at a larger firm. In a private company only a handful of senior people and the owners really know what is going on. Once Donn's team realized that we would exceed our bank line of credit and that sales were falling, everyone pulled together.

Second, Determine the Core Problem

The second crisis issue is: What exactly is the core problem to be solved? For some private companies this might be a time to bring in an investor. Related to this is knowing how bad or deep the financial crisis is. Can it be "fixed" in a short time, or should the whole company be liquidated? Don Brown, our strong willed owner, was unwilling to even consider any of these options. Instead, the key would be how our Bank would react now that our multi-million dollar credit line was not enough.

Third, Learn the Rules of the Game

If you can get past the first two steps, the need to understand the unique Rules of the Game you're in is critical. Every crisis has rules, patterns, and even language all its own. The main rule is when you are in a major crisis, you are no longer in control:
Learn to live with it.

Donn's longtime and only banker was Manufacturer's National Bank (MNB) now part of Comerica. For a small company to only have one lender, even today, is not unique. Here, in Donn's crisis, the Bank would write the Rules of the Game in a way to help save the Company.

What the Bank did first was to introduce us to Walter Heller (part of GE Capital). Heller was the innovator of what we now call asset based or secured lending. Heller took over Donn's lending and placed a security lien on all of Donn's assets.

We went to Heller's Chicago offices to learn their elaborate system for tracking and calculating our available debt, how to make debt payment draws, and how to send them all the operating and cash flow information they required. Daily, weekly, monthly.

The Heller system forced you to manage your business and live within what your cash flow generated and only that. If every company and individual was forced to do this, along with our federal and state governments, there would be no credit or debt problems in our country. (Some politician should suggest this for their next city, state or the federal budget!)

One of the hardest new Rules for Donn was that we had to pay interest to Heller at bank prime plus 7%. To prevent this interest from bankrupting Donn, MNB participated in the Heller loan by keeping half the debt and charging our old rate, prime plus 1%. This was when banks were actually direct lenders to their clients. It was also when Commercial Bankers were Bankers, unlike today's Investment Banks. So MNB only made money on the interest we paid, not on unlimited fees that banks now charge.

Keys to Managing the Donn Crisis

The Crisis Team

For a small company like Donn, there were not a lot of choices for the Team. Our President and owner, Don Brown, attended many meetings. With my boss recovering from heart surgery, I became, at age 26, the lead financial person. You learn that age and titles do not really mean much in a crisis. I was named Assistant Treasurer so I could legally sign the hundreds of documents required. The third and most important member of the Donn Crisis Team was our outside lawyer and former MNB commercial banker, Bill Kennedy who was Donn's Secretary. Bill spent a huge amount of time explaining the world of corporate finance and loan agreements to us. I learned much of the legal and technical side of business from my mentor, Bill.

Dealing with the Donn Crisis Complexity

I have learned that every business crisis has its own complexity, like the legal issues of bankruptcy or the strain on an organization to reduce cost or sell assets or all these things combined. For Donn, we went from a loose financing arrangement with our long time friendly bank to a vast set of rules, calculations and reporting required by a secured loan with Heller.

One of the first issues was to forecast realistically. Most firms forecast sales and earnings. Few make much of an effort to forecast that most illusive Business Zoo animal, Cash Flow. In the Heller secured model, still used by many financial organizations, you needed to forecast everything: Sales, Profits, Working Capital and Capital Spending.

Bottom-line, we learned to forecast. The whole company had to become experts on forecasting these components of cash flow and, they did. Because with Heller you calculated what you were allowed to have as an outstanding loan, compared that to your current actual loan and balanced the two. Daily, weekly and monthly. If your forecasting was off so was your loan amount.

Rules and Tools: Master exactly what is critical to help you get through your crisis. Here it was Heller's secured lending system and generating detail cash flow forecasts.

The other significant, complex issue we had to deal with was the Steel warehouse firm. We owed them several million dollars that we could not pay as scheduled. Our Team met the President of the warehouse and explained our goal. By working with Heller, we would take all the steel we had ordered and pay for it at the price we agreed to (which had now fallen almost in half) but we needed more time and flexibility with the payments. We agreed to monthly face-to-face meetings and weekly phone calls. There were times we had to postpone a scheduled payment because of the Heller borrowing formula but we always called them. During all this, the warehouse President and I got to know and respect each other. When USG Corporation had their Crisis years later, we again owed his company for steel and easily worked it out a second time.

Rules and Tools: In any Crisis, spend a huge amount of time communicating: in person, on the phone or email. It pays off!

Resolving the Donn Crisis

By working the Heller borrowing arrangement, Donn managed, in one and a half years to fully repay the Steel Warehouse. Manufacturers Bank reinstated the old line of credit at prime plus 1%. The construction downturn and the recession ended and Donn was back on its growth path; a decade later to be acquired by a Chicago firm called USG.

The USG Crisis

USG Corporation, founded in 1902, was the U.S. leader in the production and sale of wallboard for the construction industry. Financially, USG was a very conservative company. When construction was robust, USG generated huge profits and cash. By the mid-1980s, Sales were $3 billion, Income was $226 million and the Company was completing several, major acquisitions to become more of a building material conglomerate. The latest acquisition being a private ceilings firm from Ohio named Donn.

The USG Crisis surfaced when two buyout guys from Texas made a hostile takeover offer. USG had just recorded four years of significant growth, record earnings and a rising stock price. But the late 80's was one of the first eras of easy money to finance takeovers. Buyout firms like the Texas group would acquire a small amount of a firm's common stock, then make an offer to buy the rest, financed almost entirely with debt. Then they would break up the company and make money selling off the pieces while disassembling the budding conglomerate.

USG hired bankers and responded with what is called a leveraged recapitalization. Leverage means USG borrowed $2.5

billion from banks and issuing junk bonds. Recap meaning they paid most of the borrowed money out to their shareholders, including the Texas guys, as a huge cash dividend. USG then issued new common stock, which was worth a lot less because their risk profile had changed overnight with about four times the debt. Crain's Chicago Business said in an article, "USG's Debt Load will take its Toll." Business Week added, "USG's Remodeling may gut the House!" A clever and accurate prediction.

But what does the business media know compared to USG's senior management, its Board of Directors and investment bankers who put this deal together? After all, detailed, multi-year financial projections were used to support the new debt issuance. The construction industry was humming right along and USG was a great operating company with experienced leaders. Obviously the media would be wrong again!

Within two years the scenario had dramatically changed. Several key building material competitors had declared bankruptcy. The economic recession was deepening. The housing market sunk. USG's financial results were rapidly deteriorating as the Company announced its first quarterly loss in 90 years!
Crisis, a major financial one.

At the same time, USG's Chairman and CFO reached their mandatory retirement age. The President and Treasurer, both long time USG career people, also retired. Over 130 combined years of experience with USG and the construction industry was gone. Crisis, a major organizational one.

When you have a major financial and an organizational crisis at the same time, you have real trouble!

Approach to the USG Crisis

First, Face Reality

Initially it was very hard for USG Corporation to deal with the harsh reality of their leveraged recapitalization that added almost $3 billion of high cost debt. The Company had never borrowed much money. USG had always been an acquirer, not a takeover target for some guys from Texas.

For the first year after the recapitalization, many believed everything would turn around. Unfortunately the stock price was already dropping instead of rising as the construction slowdown occurred. USG's financial systems and incentives were not geared to its new world of massive debt and interest costs.

The Company did not forecast cash flow. And its incentive systems were tied to Operating Profit before their huge Interest bill of $800,000 a day. Like many large companies, USG had multiple levels of top management: CEOs, COOs, and Group VPs. The Company initially announced a small workforce reduction and the sale of three businesses: too little, too late.

As things got worse, the Company held daily meetings with the senior financial people, the longtime CFO and CEO.

Also in attendance were some of the newer financial people like myself from Donn and Rick Fleming, who came when USG acquired Masonite. Since we both had extensive experience in difficult situations, USG promoted us to junior Corporate Officer positions in the hopes we could come up with some "easy button" solution to this mess. There rarely is such a thing.

The immediate problem we both had was that most of the then top management was unwilling to accept the reality of how bad things could become. After one of these daily meetings, Rick and I found ourselves alone on the executive floor. We walked over to a window and from 17 floors looked down. We started to articulate our frustrations in what we would call going forward, "The Breaking Glass Theory."

The two of us felt that the office window was breaking with some external force (like billions of dollars of debt) pulling it out and us with it! We were being hurled into the air and about to drop 17 floors in a most unpleasant manner. We looked back to call for help but the executive floor was almost empty with everyone off to lunch or somewhere. A couple people might be as far away as the elevators but, they just did not have the same sense of urgency we felt, especially falling 17 floors!

Rules and Tools: Find a kindred spirit who understands and shares your view of the Crisis. Create some fun, even morbid humor like The Breaking Glass Theory, to help get you through.

In fairness, this lack of shared Reality did change with the retirements of the entire longtime, senior USG team. However, by this time, USG's stock had continued to drop to new lows. My father-in-law used to tell me that his Ohio paper must be making a mistake as they would list USG's stock at, what he liked to call, Drill Bit Prices (3/8, 1/4, etc.) But in truth, the 100 year old, proud company was becoming a penny stock.

About this time, I was named USG's new CFO and my friend, Rick, the new Treasurer. Everyone was now rushing to stand by our window! New task forces recommended a large workforce reduction. Other assets would be sold. The idea that we would incur massive shareholder dilution by having to exchange company stock for debt was becoming sadly acceptable. We even got around to whispering the potential of the B word-bankruptcy.

USG was starting to face the reality of its Crisis.

Second, Determine the Core Problem

For USG the problem was too much debt and a capital structure that needed to be fixed. All the creditors agreed that the Company was a strong, integrated operating firm with the ongoing potential for large future profits. This was in sharp contrast to some of its contemporaries. Some, like Chicago's Midway Airlines were forced into a Chapter 7 Liquidation Bankruptcy. We watched as their creditors flew all their planes, in formation, from Chicago to an Arizona plane burial ground!

To avoid that, we had to explore options for fixing our debt.

The Waiting Option: The first option was to wait till the business recovered. But in cyclical businesses you really do not know how long that can take. Meanwhile you have upset bankers and bondholders (we had now stopped all payments), shareholders with drill bit priced stock and nervous trade creditors.

Saying things would recover sounded better than explaining when that would actually happen. So our new Chairman, Gene Connolly, would tell people the fable of "Waiting for the Horse to Sing." In a far off Kingdom, the King had become disenchanted with his brother who was also his Wizard. The Wizard had not had any good tricks or advice in years due in part to consumption of the King's best wine often with the King's favorite harem ladies. So the King ordered his Wizard brother beheaded!

The Wizard said he understood but that he was sad because he was close to his greatest accomplishment that would make the King famous. The Wizard explained that he had secretly been working with the King's favorite stallion and was close to teaching the Horse to Sing! The King was excited and asked how much more time the Wizard needed. The Wizard said a year. The King said he would grant the Wizard six months. The Wizard agreed but respectfully asked if he could still have some of the King's lesser wine and women to help the creative process. The King agreed. The next day the Wizard's young apprentice reminded him that they had not been working on any such Singing Horse project, so why did the Wizard lie to the King?

The Wizard, sitting with a Harem favorite, took a long drink of good wine and thoughtfully replied to his young helper. The Wizard said that in the next six months, three things could happen: first, the King, who enjoyed the good life himself, could die; second, the Wizard planned to vastly expand his indulging on wine and women and could die himself; or third, He could actually Teach the Horse to Sing!

Rules and Tools: Create a simple, easily understood story to explain a complex option or strategic choice in your Crisis.

The Equity Investor Option: This brings us to the second option to fix the debt: we could seek a significant equity infusion from an Investor, like half a billion dollars in exchange for 25% of the Company. We put together a Who's Who of the worldwide building material industry with help from our two Investment Banks who were as excited about the potential fees on this as the King was about his Singing Horse! We talked to probably twenty-five potential investors from the U.S., Europe, and the Pacific Rim. A couple discussions got very serious, but the issues were always the same. How much money was needed to really fix the problem? How do you get all the creditors to agree?

The only Investor deal that USG publicly announced involved a Chicago firm called Zell/Chilmark, run by David Shulte, and the very successful real estate investor, Sam Zell.

Sam Zell's self-given nickname is The Gravedancer, which is meant to embody his buy low, when things are barely breathing, investment philosophy. Before you enter Sam's office in Chicago, you pass a sculpture of an open casket with a man with Sam's famous goatee dancing on it. We worked with Zell/Chilmark for several months and jointly proposed a plan to our Bank group. That Plan was rejected in three minutes. We decided not to dance with Zell/Chilmark anymore.

Somehow, I was the person elected to deliver this news. Sam and I met alone that day in his office. After disagreeing about how to proceed, Sam told me a story about box canyons.

A box canyon has a way in but no way out. He used an old West analogy that I, representing USG, would be riding off alone, without him, into a box canyon. The Bank and Bond groups, were hiding behind rocks on all sides of the Canyon. As soon as I passed, they would seal the opening and start shooting me with arrows and bullets and even throwing rocks. I would slowly bleed to death while struggling, in vain, to crawl out of the box canyon. With my last dying breath I would yell Sam! But he would be gone because USG wanted to go it alone.

In some ways this graphic story, told early in USG's three year restructuring, was accurate; it would be a long and unpleasant process with many unexpected and painful surprises.

We abandoned the equity investor option and carried on alone.

Rules and Tools: Avoid Box Canyons and Investor/Partners with scary nicknames, whether you're in a crisis or not!

The B Word Option: That brought us to USG's last two options. Both involved a version of the dreaded "B" word, bankruptcy. The preferred approach would be to seek an out-of-court deal with all the creditors and then lock it in by filing what is called a pre-packaged Bankruptcy, which a judge approves. If we were unable to get all the creditors to agree, then the Company would be forced to do a full, in court bankruptcy reorganization. It took over three years to complete the first version, a pre-packaged bankruptcy. How did we do it? In part by learning the Rules!

Third, Learn the Rules of the Game

Workout, Cases and Pain: The Wizards of finance called large financial crises, "Workouts" and called companies like USG, "Cases." This seemed to tie into medical cases because much of the language of Workouts involved body parts or activities. For example, the lowest creditor group was described, as lower than whale shit, which apparently sinks to the deepest part of the ocean where it does not receive any attention or money.

We also learned the quasi-medical phrase, "Share the Pain." In a Workout like USG's, with many layers of debtors, it was important that everyone understand how to share the pain. As USG's business declined more and more, we were still trying to determine its value to the shareholders and creditors but it was like dividing a shrinking homemade holiday pie among very hungry relatives. With the shrinking value, everyone had to give something up. The exact amount of pain you had to endure depended partly on your exact legal position in the debt structure. Secured banks-top; the whale guys-bottom.

No Secrets: The hardest Rule for many to learn was this--in the world of Workout, There are No Secrets. USG was a publicly listed stock company on the NYSE and USG's billions of debt were also publicly listed. Because of these listings, the Company had to publish financial results and make public announcements about our efforts to fix that debt.

To "help" us fix our debt, the Company's bank group and bondholders formed Credit Committees comprised of representative debt holders and their hired advisors. USG, the Committee members and their advisors all signed standard confidentiality agreements. These agreements said that each Creditor group would receive information from USG to share only within their small group, not with the public, and only for the purpose of working toward a debt restructuring with USG. In other words, the negotiations were not for public consumption. Still, we were constantly reminded, that there were No Secrets and No Confidentiality. We would meet with a Committee or their advisors on a Monday. By Tuesday, anyone in our deal or not, who wanted to know what happened, knew it. This was before Facebook but it was like everything was posted on some site as it could be repeated verbatim-often by parties not in our deal.

At first, we honestly thought people in New York were following us around in unmarked limos and using listening devices in our meetings. But the same thing happened when we had the rare meeting in Chicago in our own secure building!

We discovered there were No Secrets because some bankers, bondholders and/or their advisors were not keeping anything private. Why? Information is a valuable commodity and not just in the world of Workouts. Some people trade it constantly.

Chess vs. Checkers: The best explanation for Learning the Rules of this Game came one day at my expense. It was early in our three-year exodus and I was alone in New York having lunch with David Supino of Lazard. As USG's newly named CFO, I was trying to understand this bizarre restructuring process from David who had done this for decades. USG, again, had all these multiple groups and levels of creditors we had to satisfy to avoid a forced, in-court bankruptcy. I was explaining to David my thoughts about how to negotiate with all these parties.

My approach was this. On Star Trek's Enterprise they had a three dimensional Chess set; when you moved a piece at one level it affected pieces at the other two levels. I asked David if this was a good way to look at our situation, like a Three D Chess game. David stopped eating, spit out a piece of food, and started to shake, laugh and cry all at once. At first I thought it might be a heart attack until David screamed, "James, this is your problem! You think you are playing Chess! It's more like Checkers but half the pieces are missing or broken! There is no Board and No Rules! Now do you understand Workout!"

Rules and Tools: At times, in business or life, the phrases, No Secrets and No Rules can mean just that. Learn and be prepared.

Keys to Managing the USG Crisis

The Crisis Team

A large public company like USG with an even larger debt problem always ends up with a large Crisis Management Team. Our Internal team consisted of the newly named Chairman and President; the prime financial players were myself as the new CFO and, Rick, the new Treasurer; legal included two Assistant General Counsels, Eric and Stan. Most of us on the internal team were new to our roles, which proved to be positive. Here's how.

Creditors were often very upset with USG and its inability to live up to its financial commitments, but most of us had no significant role when the Crisis started, we were just there now trying to fix it. So we started out neutral with most people.

By contrast the formation of the External Team proved more complicated. USG needed Investment Bankers since solving this situation would require issuing more stock or debt or exchanging debt, all of which Investment Bankers do. A couple of years before

USG had hired and paid some $35 million dollars to Salomon Brothers (now part of Citicorp) and to Goldman Sachs to help us borrow all this debt which was now killing the Company.

Since we were now in trouble and could not repay this debt, we went to talk to Salomon and Goldman, with the intent of hiring and paying them, again, to clean up this mess.

Salomon said sure they were in and they personally felt bad about our situation but It's Only Business. The people who had worked with USG before at Goldman said, we don't do that kind of business anymore. We found that incredible. Bankers advise companies, and usually companies when they are in trouble, because why else would anyone want to hire an investment bank? Goldman Sachs, the premier investment bank, not in that kind of business? As USG and several other former clients would shortly discover, Goldman had just changed their business model.

Goldman had setup a separate fund, run by Goldman partners and funded with Goldman's and their clients' money to buy back at a discount, the very securities they had helped clients, like USG, sell a couple years earlier! So we did not hire Goldman to help us, but spent a huge amount of time dealing with Goldman, including two partners, who would later become Secretaries of the Treasury. Goldman and/or their Water Street Fund had "unofficial" meetings and phone calls with us and almost every other USG creditor. Goldman, through the Water Street Recovery Fund, invested about a half a billion dollars in our debt. This became exchanged for about 22% of USG's new post-workout common stock. Later, the

Fund sold their USG holdings for double their investment. Goldman, the world's "premier" bank.

No wonder we chose another Investment Banker, Lazard.

We completed the External Team with our lawyers. The firm's long time Counsel was Chicago-based Kirkland & Ellis and we added Jones Day, a firm with bankruptcy expertise.

Dealing with the USG Crisis Complexity

The Team had no shortage of complex issues including its debt structure and resulting Creditor Groups. The Creditors were split into categories based on the type of debt they held and where this debt ranked in the overall capital structure.

The Bank group had a secured position. USG had 70 banks; one third U.S., one third Japanese and one third European.

Then came newly issued 13.25% and 16% junk bonds. A lot of Creditors with different legal rights and votes to deal with.

But the most interesting aspect of this Creditor complexity was that any 3 creditors, from any combination of the various debt instruments, had the power, at any time, to throw USG into a full in-court bankruptcy.

We were working against an unknown time bomb. So we knew that it was critical that we try to move the process along and reach an out-of-court agreement. ASAP!

More Rules and Tools used to deal with USG's Crisis

When you find yourself in a Crisis which seems to have No Rules and where Wizards Advisors are giving you their expert opinions, you need a few more Rules and Tools to help you.

Rule of Three: Stated simply, if any three Wizards/Advisors or any party in our Case, independently told us to do the same thing, we had to spend a lot of time analyzing that suggestion and whether or not to do it.

This thought process evolved because we realized that, if any three people recommended the same thing, we often ended up doing it. Ultimately, the Rule of Three had application in our entire crisis since everything was up for debate. We could not have solved USG's Crisis without this Rule. This Rule works in life but only with three independent parties, not family!

The Magic 8 Ball: One day I brought a Magic 8 ball to work. That week we had a critical meeting with our own advisors as we were facing a major crossroads. This particular Crisis Team meeting was going nowhere. Our law firms and bankers could not agree on anything. So our internal USG Team had no guidance and we had a Board meeting the next day. In frustration, I picked up the Magic 8 Ball. I announced that since our Team of experts could not come up with a course of action, we would consult this ultimate source of power and wisdom. I began to formulate the Magic 8 Ball rules. We would only ask important questions of this Oracle. The question would be worded to solicit its preferred Yes/No answer. Lastly, we would abide by its answer! Our Advisors were starting to plead, don't ask the Magic 8 Ball! As I put it down, the Team came up with a consensus direction we could use. Later we would often ask the Magic 8 Ball for advice and follow it. The Magic 8 Ball had a batting average as good as any advisor group and at a fraction of the cost.

Be Proactive and Positive in Negotiations: When you owe people several billion dollars and then stop paying them, you would think they would be proactive in meeting and talking with you! Surprisingly negotiations don't always work that way. In any Crisis, there is often concern about making the first move when you have multiple parties involved.

So we began a routine that can work in many crisis situations. All our Bank/Bondholder Creditors, their Committees and their Advisor/Wizards were in NYC, so usually every Tuesday our core Crisis Team would fly there and stay two nights. Sometimes we would have meetings set up ahead and sometimes, especially in the beginning, no set meetings. Instead, upon our arrival we would call various people and invite them to lunch or dinner. We found this worked better than always trying to arrange formal meetings. We picked some favorite restaurants that often were new or trendy which we knew people would like and, of course, we always paid, as we were in Default. So yes, we bribed people as covered in our upcoming chapter, Lunches and Dinners.

Being Positive with Humor and Thank Yous: Early on, one of our Investment Bankers told us that during a Workout, members of a company's Crisis Team usually develop some very bad habits, like drinking or drugs. We tried to avoid this and take our minds off some of the darkness with humor. Cartoons with USG or one of our names would just appear.

One cartoon shows three fish standing outside of a USG labelled fish bowl on fire. One fish says "Thank God we all made it out in time. Course we are now equally screwed!"

We also tried to be extremely courteous in an often rude world. Whenever we made even small progress we would leave late night thank you calls to the group we had met with and to our own Advisors. Little things often are remembered.

But USG had one more kind of positive power working for it.

Praying for Sheetrock and the Parking Nuns

Praying for Sheetrock

A year into our Crisis, a National Book award novel came out using USG's registered trademark. Praying for Sheetrock is the story of a Southern family whose house was to be improved under a government program that ran out of money just before the drywall or Sheetrock was to be installed. They prayed and there was a happy ending. We decided praying might not be a bad idea.

One day our head outside lawyer, Frank, was with us at Lazard offices at Rockefeller Center. We had finished more meetings with our Creditor groups and we were waiting, with our Lazard friend Doug, for a response. But this afternoon Frank, a Notre Dame product, decided waiting was not enough.

Frank led me and our Treasurer, Rick, on a forced march to the impressive St. Patrick's Cathedral on Madison. We walked in and followed Frank as he genuflected in the aisle, went to a pew, said a silent prayer, went over to their wall of candles, lit one, put money in the candle donation box, went over to what we used to call the poor box, put money in the poor box, genuflected again and went back outside.

This would have been easy for anyone who was raised Catholic. My friend Rick was not. He had trouble with the genuflecting concept. But Rick really had trouble with the money in the donation box part. You see, that day Rick had only twenties!

Since he was last in our procession through the massive Church, he also had no wingman. Rick did the only thing he could do, he put the big bucks in the donation boxes. We made this trip several more times over our three year Workout. But at all times, Rick made sure he had a number of $1 bills.

The Parking Nuns

We also had divine support in Chicago.

Since the mid-1800's, the Sisters of the Good Shepherd have been located near Wrigley field, home of the Chicago Cubs. Old-timers called their order the Parking Nuns, because for decades the Sisters had parked cars during Cubs games at their Convent.

In December of 1992, we finally had all the stars aligned to complete a consensual out-of-court restructuring. All the Creditor groups had agreed to our Plan. At the last minute, one group, the lowly 16% bondholders said no. This was our third year-end in Default. The Company, its employees and the Crisis Team were exhausted.

At that very moment, the head investment banker Advisor for those same 16% bondholders sent me a holiday gift. A turkey that was shipped frozen and then must be eaten within three days. For the next three days we would be dealing with our equally tired Board of Directors, so I had a surplus turkey. I offered it to my Administrative Assistant, Denyse. She said no, but had an idea.

Her Professional Secretary group, was making a donation that year to a group of nuns who helped battered women. They were the Sisters of the Good Shepherd.

The Sisters facility is only a few miles north of us in Chicago. I drove over, leaving the turkey and my business card, just in case of food poisoning.

At the same time, my personal bank, made a mistake which caused me some embarrassment. A senior banking officer shows up at my office and gives me a $1,000 check, like a fee refund, to make me happy. I tell him I did not request a payment, I just want the problem fixed. He insists. I tell him fine, I will take the check and donate it to charity. I drive back to the Sisters with a $1,000 check in our Christmas card.

In the card, I ask the Sisters to pray for our families and USG Corporation.

The Sisters write back that my requests will be in their Novena Mass prayers the following week of Christmas.

Three weeks later, USG had a Deal.

USG's Crisis Solution and Epilogue

Overall Time Table of Crisis

- USG defaulted on the Bank loans and Bonds in December, 1990.
- A Creditors agreement was reached in January, 1993.
- A prepackaged, consensual reorganization plan was filed with the bankruptcy court in March, 1993. USG exited bankruptcy in May, 1993.

The Final Financial Solution ended up like this:

- The Bank debt received 100% of their face value.
- The Junk Bonds received 97% of the new Common Stock.
- The old Common Shareholders, including the large employee group, received an unheard of 3% of the new Common Stock, which still resulted in a massive dilution of their value.
- USG retained ten of their existing Directors or two-thirds of the Board; a most unusual occurrence for a Company that exchanged 97% of their Common Stock to their debt-holders. Within two years the Goldman/Water Street Fund stock ownership and their two Directors were gone. We had prayed for that day as well!

The new Capital structure provided the Company with flexibility and future opportunity. The total Debt was reduced by half. The new Common Stock started trading on the NYSE at $10 and within a couple years was selling for $30.

Any holder of Bank Debt or Junk Bonds, which were exchanged into new USG stock, who held their USG debt for the whole Crisis, received back 100% of their investment.

Epilogue

When asked how I personally dealt with the long USG Crisis, I find myself telling the story of Karl Wallenda. The Wallendas were a multi-generation family who walked the high wire. Their performances were unique because they worked without a net and they would build a seven person family pyramid on the wire.

Karl Wallenda was the head of the family and had taught his whole family to walk the wire. Later in his life, he performed a number of solo walks. One clear day, walking between two buildings in Puerto Rico, Karl fell to his death. His family reported that he had acted strangely for days before that walk, extensively questioning family members who were making the preparations, as he had taught them to do. He seemed worried about every detail. His family concluded that Karl had violated the first rule of walking the wire, the rule he had taught all of them: Focus on getting to the other side.

In the end, he had focused on "not falling" and he died.

The USG Crisis Team focused on saving the Company. USG had been around a long time and was a great operating organization, with fine values and loyal employees.

USG was worth saving.

We were going to get to the other side and we did.

Lessons Learned from Crisis Management

There are problems in business and life and there are Crises.
Learn to tell them apart. Sometimes this takes experience.

A Financial Crisis occurring with an Organizational Crisis equals a real mess!

Most problems or crisis in life or business involve money or the lack of it.

All Organizations, business or not, will have a Crisis due to a combination of internal and external factors.

Although you cannot avoid a Crisis, there are ways you can help Manage and Survive it with the help of Rules and Tools.

When you Approach a Crisis these steps are critical:
- – Face the true Reality quickly and as a Team
- – Determine the real Core Problem to solve
- – Explore all Options to solve your Crisis
- – Learn the unique Rules and Language of the Crisis

The Keys to Managing any Crisis include:
- – Form a small but adaptable Crisis Team
- – Deal with your Crisis' unique Complexity issues
- – Stay on the High Wire until you have resolved the Crisis

Rules and Tools to Assist in a Crisis:

- Master the skills, like forecasting, to survive a Crisis
- Spend a huge amount of time communicating
- Create stories to explain complex concepts or options
- Avoid box canyons and people with scary nicknames
- Decide at times if you are playing Chess or Checkers
- No Secrets and No Rules can mean just that; be ready
- Meet with key outside parties over lunches and dinners
- Remember the Rule of Three as a guide to action
- Use Magic 8 Balls or whatever device helps
- Be Proactive and Positive even in difficult times
- Use Humor and Thank you calls extensively
- Sometimes even Praying or Parking Nuns can help
- Always have small bills or change in a church

And always Remember to Focus on getting across the Wire and out of your Crisis; don't think about falling or you will!

4. Lunches and Dinners

(Key to Business and Life)

Importance of Breaking Bread

Over years of Lunches and Dinners I:

– Learned more about business and life than anywhere else
– Solved more problems and made more deals with friends and foes
– Spent more helpful time mentoring young people

I could go on but let's start with my own dining education.

Dining with Europeans

Despite the issues that I had with some of my Donn European executive friends, like the occasional Management Fraud, they had an incredible ability to negotiate business matters while enjoying the good life. In Europe, food and wine are of huge importance. Business meetings are scheduled after plans are in place for Lunches and Dinners. Important visitors and guests are taken to the finest places for lavish dining. Time and cost receive little attention; it's the experience that is important. And with our European friends it was not just about enjoying the meal and our company, it was often about using these relaxed moments of fellowship to ask those of us from the corporate headquarters for something!

Lunch in Paris, for example, often followed a meeting with our French banks or our local accounting firm. Our French President Chris and his Controller Arnaud did the hosting. The meal started with a light wine like Sancerre accompanied by some wonderful starter. A fish such as sea bass with Chablis would be the main course. Then somehow our French friends decided that all Americans loved chocolate so the wait staff would bring a giant crock of mousse de chocolat.

It was at this point, before we were even offered espresso, when we, simple Americans, were stuffed and in love with all things French, that one of our hosts would bring something up. It could be that the local accountants had mentioned some new tax loophole that could reduce their personal tax bill. We might be together the rest of the day but these matters needed to be discussed and agreed upon right now! More challenging than this were the dinners and requests at our next stop in Germany.

The Grand Master of Lunches and Dinners

Germany was the location of Donn's European headquarters. Here also was Donn's worldwide grand master of the good life, our European President, Branco. From 1968 to the sale of Donn in 1986, his business grew from zero to four locations with $50 million in sales and $2 million in net income-a huge success.

If the European Donn Presidents were treated like Kings, Branco was the Emperor of the Kingdom. And he provided me with a lifetime of both business and life adventures.

On one of my first solo trips to Germany, I was told we were going out to eat with important customers. I thought this would be great for me to observe the real business, especially in Germany where many people spoke some English. At 4 pm the European Controller, Gunther, and I were summoned to Branco's office. He had decided we needed to stop working. He poured us each a Campari and soda from his office bar. Alcohol #1.

We then drove to a remote restaurant outside of Dusseldorf. In the bar we drank the two types of German beer they had on tap, an Alt and a Pilsner. Alcohol #2.

We joined the customers for dinner, which began with white asparagus and white German Franken wine. Alcohol #3.

By the main meat course I am relaxed with an excellent French red wine, Alcohol #4. I asked the group for the local name of the delicious meat. In German they struggled and debated the proper English word. And then several shouted: BAMBI! Yes, our beloved childhood movie hero, Bambi. Then they illustrated this for me by placing both hands over their heads in antler type fashion. Technically, I later learned it was wild reindeer but I do not think Rudolph was as well known.

We then adjourned to the bar and had strong after dinner drinks like cognac and brandy, which the group assured me are what they call digestifs which aid with your digestion. Alcohol #5. Then somehow we drove back to Dusseldorf to the famous hotel where Branco was residing and I was staying. We had a final bottle of French Champagne in his suite. Alcohol #6.

I am not sure he asked me for any help that night as I probably would have agreed to anything to stop drinking. Plus I would not have remembered the next day. But what I really learned from Branco is how to get people to help you without ever asking...

One dreadful day, the local German tax authorities came to audit our Donn Germany business which paid all of Branco's compensation. They decided that since Branco was in charge of all four of Donn's European businesses, some of his total compensation and expenses should be charged to the other three units. They decided to disallow our German company tax deductions and to levy a personal dividend tax on Branco! And for four years!

This was not good. Not good for our German company that would have to pay for the disallowed costs plus penalty plus interest. But really not good for Branco who would have to personally pay for this so-called dividend. And remember, as a Donn European King or Emperor, these were not modest amounts! But big bucks!

We were granted a few weeks to provide them our answer or else all forms of German tax Hell would occur. So we decided to bring in help, our U.S. and German CPA tax experts.

Our U.S. tax partner and manager accompanied me to Germany. With our European Controller, we went to meet their German counterparts the next day. Branco was supposed to join us for the all-day meeting. He showed up at the restaurant for Lunch, naturally. Then ordered, against my advice, some expensive wine and the short, alcohol-free meal I had hoped for became a several hour affair. The U.S. and local tax people enjoyed themselves immensely, and their host Branco was, as always, the Grand Master of ceremonies or in this case, Lunch.

No worthwhile tax business was discussed, just stories.

I asked Branco to join us for our group wrap-up meeting after lunch to help prepare for the next day's meeting with the German tax authorities. This way Branco would be familiar with our strategy involving both the Company and his personal liability. But meetings were not his thing; Branco vanished. We often said he was like an eagle flying high above us all.

That evening, our European Controller, Gunther, and I took our two U.S. tax guys out for dinner. I planned a brief American style meal with just enough alcohol to relax the group for the next day's meeting. The dinner worked out fine until the end.

Out of nowhere Branco showed up and announced he was buying a drink for his new American friends at Dusseldorf's most famous nightclub, which was on the way to our hotel. I suggested that this best be deferred until after our critical meeting the next day, but Branco grabbed my two U.S. tax experts and led us all on a march to the nightclub. It was only 9pm on a weeknight, so the nightclub was empty. We sat down and I thought this may work out if we only had one drink. Even I, after my years with Europeans, could not anticipate what happened next.

Out of nowhere, again, appear three beautiful young German ladies. I recognize one from our German company who was dating our European Controller; another was a good friend of hers I had met on some other Branco organized event, and a third I did not know. As if by magic, all of us Americans are being dragged to the dance floor! An hour later I suggest to Branco we should wrap the evening up with our big day coming.

A second hour goes by, more drinking, dancing and talking with the beautiful German ladies. Then Branco stands up. He seems to wave his hand. The music stops. The three beautiful ladies vanish. The U.S. tax guys and I are standing on an empty street. Branco is telling us good luck with the meeting and he knows we will do a great job. Branco vanishes again. Now it's just us three Americans standing outside of our hotel.

The next day the two U.S. tax experts fought the German tax authorities to the death on behalf of their new close friend, Branco. The Donn German company paid a moderate tax and penalty and agreed to allocate Branco's cost throughout Europe. Branco was not charged anything. Our U.S. and German tax experts insisted he not be taxed!

After all, how can you tax a phantom, especially one who was the Grand Master of Lunches and Dinners?

Seating, Flow and Wine

I learned a few other critical things about dining from my European friends.

Seating

Before we sat down at even the rare, simple lunch, the head local person acted as the host and instructed everyone where to sit. The most important visitor or business guest was seated to the right of the host. If it was a large dinner, there might be a second acting host at each end of the table. Guests from the same company or visitors from the U.S. were divided and did not sit together. All this sounds basic and simple but it is not. Without ever asking, I was put in charge of seating for our U.S. events. In a private company like Donn, it was important that we not seat the family owners together. At USG Corporation, there were rivals who really did not like to sit near each other. Careers can be made or lost at dinners, so watch where you are seated.

Flow

Next the Flow of a dining experience must be managed. If time is tight, you order a starter and wine for the table. If the meal is meant to be leisurely, you explain that to the waitperson and you explain that a good tip will materialize if your needs are met. If a guest is confused on what to order, you help. If people claim not to be hungry, you suggest sharing. If people love food, you suggest sharing several courses. You know how much wine is left without looking at the bottles and you order another bottle before you are empty. Depending on the size and group, even if no one claims to want dessert, you order one or two for the table. Flow during the meal is critical to a successful Lunch or Dinner and the resulting business that can occur.

Wine

We end this section where many meals succeed or fail, with the Wine. Today most people prefer Wine to hard alcohol or beer with their meals. Remember what type of wine friends and business associates like to drink. My European friends did all this naturally and people loved it. And since someone has to order the Wine, you need to learn the basics.

This is especially important for young business women. As you move up and are in charge of a Dinner, you need to know how to do this or how to ask the server to help you while maintaining the aura of being in control. You do not need to master all wines. There are endless, excellent wines from every corner of our country and the world. But, what you can learn are a couple of domestic Chardonnays and Cabernets that are often found on most wine lists and are within the budget of the event.

If you can learn the rules of Seating, manage the Flow of the meal and deal with the Wine, you too, can become a Master of Lunches and Dinners. Let's look at how you can use these new skills to help yourself and others.

Dining with Wolves and Rats and other Adversaries

While I was in the middle of the USG Financial Crisis, I was describing to a friend the type of people I was working with and against. As I touched on some of my adversaries' better personal qualities, like lying and going back on their word, I also described some of their lunchroom antics.

Some of the Wizards had unusual eating habits including:

– Picking up and staring at a number of sandwiches.
– Or better yet smelling several items before choosing.
– Once someone even took a bite and put it back.

Our friend was shocked by all this and said it sounded like I was working with a pack of Wolves!

That weekend I became fascinated with Wolves after watching a TV special. Friends gave me Wolf books and I even started to send out Wolf Holiday cards. So what is the big deal about Wolves? The big deal, as verified in scientific studies, is:

- Wolves have been here over 1 million years
- Wolves are very intelligent, very social and follow rules
- Wolves prefer to live away from humans and there is little evidence that they rarely ever attack people or eat Red Riding Hood
- The female lead chooses where they live, when they move, can lead the hunt and can assign nursing her pups to someone else
- Siblings separated as pups can recognize their brother or sister's howl for the rest of their often 10 year lifespan
- A pack can travel across a snow covered area and walk in each other's steps so no one knows how many have passed

Now how many groups of Advisor Wizards or corporate teams can live up to the level of Wolves? Not very many.

But I have also studied Rats.

In Latin the word Rat means "of unknown origin" since they have been around forever. Rats only reside near humans, they eat our waste, only live a year and carry disease including the original plague. Rats can swim under water for a mile. Rats can chew their way through a concrete block. And Rats eat anything, often after smelling and touching it!

I went back to our friend and said that no, I did not work with a lot of Wolves but I did work with a lot of Rats!

So why and how should you dine with Rats and other adversaries? First, you should act like a European lone wolf. A great dinner, with proper Seating, Flow and Wine is a perfect way to learn something about the other person. You can see if you have any similar views or common ground on anything in the deal. Dinner is also the perfect way to make some progress and to let someone believe they are critical to the process. You can best reinforce this either one-on-one or in a small wolf pack.

Dining with adversaries has been extremely useful to me in many other internal and external problem areas. When Donn was acquired by USG, we used Dining to help bring the diverse Donn, USG, and Masonite groups together. To move forward, we all had to work together immediately. For example, we had to create a common sales order/billing system so we could sell our ceiling tile and grid together as a package. To kick off projects like this, I would arrange a series of meetings with the Cleveland Donn people and the Chicago USG people, most of whom had never met each other.

The meeting started, not in the office, but with a mandatory dinner the night before in Chicago. We would often start with a shellfish starter platter, then wine and food, and shared dessert. Some of the people got along great as the dinner went on and in those cases, the meeting the next day was seamless. Sometimes dinner was not so good which meant I had figure out and deal with the real troublemakers, even sadly if they were my own Donn people. Bottom line, if people are acting badly at a wonderful dinner organized by a European trained junior master of ceremonies like me, they will only act worse as you try to move the project or the separate businesses together. Sometimes it was like watching someone take their dinner steak knife and cut their own throat (read career) while you and others watched.

You learn a lot at Dinners.

I would also do one-on-one Dinners with some of the senior USG financial people. In the beginning, I was the new kid asking them out. Then when I was promoted to CFO over some longtime USG people, I would use the Dinners as a way to see if we could find common ground or to form what I call, A Separate Peace (a book by John Knowles). In this context, the dinners sometimes worked well and so did our roles going-forward. With others, I quickly learned that it would never be an ideal reporting relationship.

But you find out much more in a long lunch or dinner than by working together in the office for months. Some of these rivals or potential adversaries like the Treasurer Rick or the Gypsum Controller Ray became great financial teammates and even lifelong friends. The initial meals alone helped a lot.

On other occasions, Dinners have allowed me to get a Deal finalized. In every Acquisition, Divestiture, Financing etc., there are always open issues. Again, two people, have a better chance of getting something done over a Dinner. An office also makes it too convenient for those Wizard Lawyers or Bankers to join you and this usually does not provide closure. At a Dinner with just two principal negotiators, you will either make progress and get the Deal done or you will learn that it is never going to happen.

Dining with the Kids

Throughout my career, and to this day, I do a lot of Dining with the Kids. Kids is a term I have used forever to describe anyone younger than I am; this now includes much of the population. In my formal working days, the young people were often one, two or three levels below me in whatever company I was with. Usually Dining was Lunch and almost always away from the office. The office, especially an executive office, is not a good place to try to talk with younger people. No one, not even the executives, feel comfortable there.

Nowadays it can also be the increasingly popular coffee break at Starbucks. And almost always, I buy unless they just got the new job of their dreams and they are trying to thank me for some bit of advice. I tell the Kids to buy when I am old.

The key to successful Dining with the Kids is to get them to talk voluntarily. This is in stark contrast to certain Human Resource types who take people out and drill them with a series of life altering questions - Where do you want to be in three and five years? Answer: Who the Hell knows? How do you really feel about your boss or peer? Answer: What?

Usually the Kids are worried about something that affects them right now. Sometimes it is even about their boss or peer but they have to decide to tell you. This does not mean you cannot ask questions, even somewhat leading questions, but only after you have built up at least a thin layer of trust and respect. To build that trust you usually need to have more than one lunch. You also need to learn to guard, and not act on, what you are told in private.

Gaining the trust of the young people in your organization is very important because then, and only then, can you mentor, advise and develop them. This is critical as I believe that personnel development is not a Human Resource function but rather should be led by the business and functional managers as well as company executives. H.R. has a role to play and can provide a number of support activities like skills development, diversity programs or tools like job postings. But H.R. should not take the lead or act like the sole puppet master of people.

That said, I found some Tools of my own to help make the Kids relax and be more willing to discuss a wide range of career and development topics while Dining. Let's take a look at some of the more popular ones.

Salt, Pepper and Sugar packs: Restaurants have always provided me with the ultimate in visual aids, the condiment holders right in front of us. Many times a Kid's concerns dealt with organization issues- their department's structure, their group's role versus other groups, combining or downsizing groups. The Salt, Pepper, and Sugar packs allowed me to create unlimited combinations to visually show them what was occurring and, at times, let them move the pieces around as well. The largest container, usually Salt, would become the head of their department or group. Since Sugar usually comes in three or more colors or brands, it was used to represent a number of their peers. Pepper, I must say, was often left for their protagonist or tormentor or often those pesky H.R. people who could make your eyes water with too much help.

Ranking on a Scale of 1 to 10: Often the best way to get someone's real feelings is to ask them to do a Ranking. For example, if their job seems to be the issue, you ask them to Rank it against their vision of the perfect job. I find it best to label the extremes. So a 1 or 2 would be comparable to having oral surgery. A 10 is like working on a beach for a lot of money. If their answer is from the middle up, you can help them by finding ways to make the job or their view of the job better.

Comparative Ranking or the Continuum Scale: A critical refinement of the 1 to 10 Ranking is to ask the young person to see themselves and others along a line which shows their comparative rank or position on a type of graduated scale. Here again it's best to lay out the scale and place someone on it for them. This works very well when helping someone see how their personality or style compares to others.

If the concern is how outgoing or assertive the person is, I draw the scale from very shy/introverted at one end to very outgoing/aggressive at the other. And then I place one or more people they know well on the scale often as close to the extreme ends as possible. Then I have the person place themselves on the same scale. Depending on how close they came to my view of them, I might simply agree or move them a little to encourage them if they seem too self-critical. I have used this system to illustrate many points: technical knowledge, visibility, promotability, presentation skills. Once the person sees where they fit, you can help them.

Rating the 3 C's: Over the years many different books and methods have been used to assess careers and job satisfaction. I ask the Kids to think about and rate their job based on these 3 C's. Confidence: how sure are you that you have the required skills or knowledge to do the job? Commitment: do you really believe in what you are trying to accomplish in this role? And finally Control: how much real control/power/authority do you have to do the job? If people have none of these, they and the job are in trouble. Two out of three, like Meatloaf said in the song, ain't bad and, it's probably more the norm. But if and when you can see your way to achieving all three, you and the job will shine.

During the Donn Financial Crisis, when I was in my 20's, I had a total Commitment to save the Company and, with my boss on medical leave, I had almost total Control. I had very little idea as to what I was doing, so Confidence was an issue. During the USG Financial Crisis I was older, had done more, and had all 3 C's. But talk about how those 3C's change! Sometimes it's you, sometimes it is the specific job or sometimes it's some other circumstance. The goal is to feel good about all 3 C's in your current role or the one you seek to move into.

Cats versus Dogs: I this learned from my friend John, who upon meeting my son, Mike, declared that he was a Dog! John explained that most of us, when meeting people, act like Cats or Dogs.

Picture a cocktail hour at a work seminar where you know some people, might want to meet others but want to stay clear of some others. A Dog enters the room and runs up to everyone they know or don't know wagging their tail (extending handshakes). They do this almost at random until they run out of new people.

A Cat walks around the outside of the room studying the occupants. When it is ready, and only when it's ready, the Cat heads for the one, single person or group they find interesting or worthy. When they tire of this person or group, and Cats always do tire, they repeat this focused search or just leave!

So we ask the Kids how they would act in some situations. There is no right answer but it can help a young person see themselves in a clearer light. It can also reveal something about the young person's confidence level. It takes a lot more energy and willingness to be rejected, to be a Dog at times. On the other hand, many people consider Cats to be lone Wolves or lacking social skills.

At times, we share with the Kids some of my own experiences with Cats and Dogs. Shortly after USG acquired Donn, we were invited to our first couples USG social event. At that event, all the Donn people were Cats on the edge of the group as long as they could be. At other times, as CFO of my companies I organized meetings of all the worldwide financial people. Since I was the presumed boss and host, I was a super Dog trying to introduce people to each other and talking to everyone.

What I try to tell young people is that there are times to be both, a Dog or a Cat. Part of the transition comes from confidence (higher positions), some with comfort about your company's culture (longevity) and some just from living and working. The key thing is you must keep growing into a wise big Dog or big Cat!

We can learn a lot from our animal friends to help us with Lunches and Dinners to promote our own careers or to help the many Kids we meet along the way.

Lessons Learned from Lunches and Dinners

Dining in small groups is a critical part of learning and teaching business and life lessons so:

- – When you are the Kid, go, watch, listen and learn.
- – When you are the Boss, go, advise and teach.

Careers can be lengthened or shortened based on who one sits near and how one acts at Lunches and Dinners.

Mastering the art of the great meal, Seating, Flow, and Wine will add value and enjoyment-in business and in life.

People want to be remembered for something; if you learn to be a Master of Dining, people will remember you forever.

If corporate teams worked as effortlessly and as well as a Wolf pack, they would always windup as winners.

Dining with Adversaries can lead to solutions and friendships; but be wary of Rats and the infamous Pepper Shakers (H.R.).

But the best is Dining with the Kids, finding tools to help and learning to listen; you can actually learn a lot!

5. True Selling

(Real Marketing Superstars)

What is Selling Anyway?

Almost everyone in the world is involved in Selling. Kids sell their wants and needs to their parents; spouses to each other; workers to their bosses; and bosses reluctantly to their Boards and Wall Street. Without Selling, nothing much ever happens. Without Selling, we do not need manufacturing plants and we certainly do not need accountants. But even though everyone sells, what we call Sales and Marketing varies a lot.

My wife sold office furniture systems (like Steelcase). For decades, customers had annual contracts that dealt with pricing; you did not exactly sell, you serviced the account based on the contract. Nowadays, the annual contracts have been replaced with fierce bidding on every small or large project. Now it's dog-eat-dog Selling, not gentlemanly servicing the account.

My son, Mike, works in the wire and cable and electrical supply industry. As an inside Salesperson he often negotiates both the buy from the manufacturer and the sell to the customer. To me, this always seemed to be more of a trading kind of selling since the outside Sales people were more involved in the relationship than the pricing details.

In the building material industry with Donn and USG, all the Sales and Marketing people used to talk constantly about how hard it was to sell! But these products were commodities that people needed to build houses or commercial buildings.

A European policeman I got to know during our Management Fraud situation once told me that our building products were purchased because people needed them, not because we sold them. Nowadays, a huge amount of these building products go to the big box stores like Lowe's. These powerful buyers tell you what, when and how much they will pay. They buy, but do you really sell?

Over the years I have often told salespeople that even us simple non-sales types are involved in types of Selling. For example, the legal staff is often involved in litigation and has to defend the company by selling some business concept to a judge. Financial people, as discussed in The USG Crisis, have to try to sell the long term viability of their company to Wall Street and all those nasty creditor groups.

So, my point to the Sales people is that sometimes it is harder to sell the concept of the whole company in these cases than to sell some wonderful, useful building material product!

Yet, for all this, you still hear or read stories about people who can sell anything. Like ice to the Eskimos.

So let's look at some of the Master Salespeople and Marketers I have met.

Donn Marketing Superstars

Walter was the General Manager of Donn Scandinavia which covered the northern European, Nordic countries. Frank had started in inside sales and became the VP of Sales/Marketing for Donn Canada. From thousands of miles apart they each developed a unique and successful approach to marketing our products.

Walter, the Promoter:

The area called Scandinavia covers a half dozen countries in northern Europe, Iceland, and Greenland. This area is one third of the U.S. with one tenth our population. Walter was headquartered outside of Stockholm. Donn Scandinavia did not manufacture any products; they were all imported from other Donn locations primarily in Europe. So Walter had no ability to easily customize products for his local markets. Walter also did not benefit from the full profit of a sale since the producing Donn location included a transfer price markup. Walter also had huge transportation costs to get products to his customers.

Regardless, Donn Scandinavia grew as fast in sales and net profits as any other international location, even with the built-in obstacles Walter faced. And Walter overcame them fast and did it with a unique Marketing flair.

Whenever we would get the senior business people together, Walter would hand out some new Marketing promotional item. A black leather change purse with the Donn logo. A brown leather note card holder with your name engraved with the Donn logo. He visited a tomb in Egypt, saw an ancient stone carving with the word DONN, and had holiday cards made with a picture of him covering all except the DONN letters. All the other business units would beg him for a sample and then they would copy the item for their own customers. Walter did all this with no staff.

But Walter's best effort was The Book of Ceilings. Before the internet and access to everything, he created a book of ceilings over the history of time. Rome to the new Stockholm airport; stone engraved, to wood carved; pictures not words.

In typical Walter style, he brought this to a business meeting and handed one around. Everyone, including people who had been in the building business for decades, was amazed. The Book of Ceilings also had very few advertisements about the Donn company, just a small preamble, in English, explaining that this was a gift from Donn Scandinavia and of course, from Walter. We ordered thousands and sent them all over the world.

Frank, the Specialty Guy

Canada is as large in land area as the U.S. with one tenth of our population in a handful of scattered, major cities. Donn Canada, was located near Toronto, Ontario, and, as our first international business, grew in sales and profits every year.

Unlike Donn Scandinavia, Canada manufactured not only the standard suspended ceiling grids but a number of Specialty Ceilings as well. The Specialty Ceilings often sold for much higher prices, but were used in a more limited fashion: the lobby of a building, an airport concourse, an executive floor. You have walked under these shiny, colorful metal pans in buildings and maybe even in your favorite casino!

Specialty Ceilings required an architect or designer to specify them for a project. In addition, Specialty Ceiling projects were scarce and hard to secure. It was also harder to be profitable with specialty products because they were made on shorter, less automated equipment, unlike the standard ceiling grids that were produced on high-speed production lines.

In spite of these drawbacks, every year Donn Canada, under Frank, always sold more Specialty Ceilings than the much bigger Donn U.S. business. They also became, without the large research and engineering group that we had in the U.S., the inventor and, to this day, the main manufacturer of many of USG Interiors' Specialty Ceilings sold worldwide.

When USG (drywall building products), in one of their expansion modes acquired Masonite (forest, wood products), they found they had also acquired a Specialty Ceiling business called Integrated Ceilings. A couple years later, when USG brought Donn, someone at headquarters decided that this small Masonite business would fit better with USG Interiors.

But instead of letting anyone from Donn or Donn Canada run this one, headquarters decided that Integrated Ceilings would remain separate with an up-and-coming gypsum drywall person in charge. Integrated Ceilings was in southern California and worked primarily with architects who were called upon by their specialty representatives. That successful network was abandoned in favor of using our USG Interiors commodity sales people. In addition, Integrated Ceilings only made unique products, custom designed for each job and produced by small, outside tool shops. So what did we do? We created a standard product line and brought all the production in house, spending a lot on tooling.

Integrated Ceilings had always made profits. Now, we lost money and shut it down within two years. The General Manager was promoted to another business. Selling Specialty Ceilings was not so easy. Unless you were a Donn Marketing Superstar.

Coming to Headquarters

Integrated Ceilings was the story of a big company wrecking havoc on a Marketing success. This story is about a big company wrecking havoc on a successful Salesperson.

After my days as CFO at USG, I was asked to become the President of the USG Interiors business (including Donn). For me, the most fun part of this role was meeting our customers. Some of the most challenging to handle were on the East coast. On a visit with one of our largest East coast customers, their President asked me into his office and closed the door. Usually this is not good. But he wanted to tell me that he was informed that my sister group, U.S. Gypsum, was promoting and relocating their local salesperson to the Chicago Headquarters. We will call her, Diane.

The East Coast customer President is telling me what a wonderful salesperson Diane had become, and how they will really miss her. He also said that when she first came on their account a number of his longtime, hard-nosed guys were not sure this would work, but now they all think Diane is great. Later that day, I was on a job site with one of his top salesmen, another fast talking East coast guy; he tells me the same story about Diane. The next day at another location, a third guy says the same thing. Now I am really listening because of my Rule of Three.

A few weeks after my return to headquarters, I made sure I met this Diane person just to say hello and tell her that her old customers were singing her praises. I asked her how the first month had gone since moving to headquarters. She hesitated. I then added that the customer President insisted I take her to lunch on him (a small falsehood).

We went to lunch a week or so later. After the small talk, I again asked about her relocation to headquarters and how it was going. She tells me she is not sure. She is concerned about how some of her new peers and bosses seem to react to her. I ask Diane to describe a typical week in detail since starting her new job here in Chicago.

She tells me how she has a new and large geographic territory, with a lot of sales people and customers she does not know. So she is trying to do what she thinks is best and what worked for her on the East coast. She is traveling 4 to 5 days a week in this new territory meeting everyone and is rarely in the Chicago Headquarters office. I calmly explain to her that this is her problem. The people at headquarters care first about the people at headquarters, then a distant second about what happens in the "field" where all the customers and sales really occur. In addition, the people at headquarters expect her, as a new person, to constantly update the rest of them about what is going on out there in the field. But to do that she needs to change her schedule, at least initially. I suggest that she spend two days a week here at headquarters just walking around, going to lunch, attending meetings, so the headquarters people will get to know her, and she can help them and their bosses with her stories from the field. She thought this was crazy, but said she understood what I meant since some people seemed surprised she was out in the field so much. I offered to meet for lunch again and I think we did. Within a few years, I was gone from headquarters, and a few years later so was Diane. I hope she is out in the field selling something and still being loved by her tough customers wherever they are!

Big firms and their headquarters do not destroy everything in their paths, but they often have a real problem dealing with anything that does not fit into their cultural vision of their world. USG was successful for decades with mass-produced structural building products that did not require much creative selling or marketing like Specialty Ceilings. Even the people who sold the products became more homogenous and interchangeable. So individuals with their own views on Selling, like Diane, did not fit in so easily.

 Let's wrap up with the story of a different kind of Salesman.

Selling a Hotel to Holiday Inn

Donn and Modular Housing, the Prelude

Since the early 1950's when it was founded by Don Brown, Donn Corporation had manufactured suspended ceiling systems. But Mr. Brown kept looking to add new products that involved either our steel raw materials, our roll-forming manufacturing expertise, or items used in the construction market.

Modules or factory built housing first became popular in the late 1960's. The federal government authorized the Department of Housing and Urban Development (HUD) to support this concept with the idea that it would result in more affordable buildings particularly for housing. (The U.S. government has been messing with housing long before Fannie May and the real estate and mortgage crisis of recent years!)

Mr. Brown saw this as a great opportunity to get his young company in on a trend that had some tie-in to Donn's manufacturing base and the construction end-market. As an engineer, he oversaw the design of several modules and built a prototype. But to tool up a factory would cost a lot; Donn needed a partner. A partner with money.

Jones & Laughlin Steel (J&L) was a giant company in its day. They produced steel. They had money. And in the late 1960's, everyone wanted in on the Modular housing boom. Brown had the technology and the prototype. J&L would provide the finances and invested $1 million (1968 dollars) for which they received 49% of the project, a new modular plant, and a partnership called Jal-Donn Building Systems. A low-income apartment project was built near J&L's base in Pittsburgh. Even the Secretary of HUD, George Romney (yes, father of Mitt) visited for a photo op. Hopefully all this free public relations was valuable for J&L, because this first and only project lost a lot of their money. Mr. Brown then bought out J&L's interest for $1, that's one 1970 dollar. He kept the technology and the modular plant. But now he needed another partner.

Donn ended up with two different partners and partnerships over a couple years. Each partner brought a different ingredient to the mix. The first partner was a local, successful apartment developer who had worked on government projects, and had land and money to restart the renamed modular plant. One expensive apartment project later, and he was gone taking the apartment building with him. Mr. Brown again kept full ownership of the technology and the modular plant.

The second partner owned a local, successful engineering firm and was connected to a well-known restaurant group, which had decided to enter the budget motel business. One expensive, budget motel project later and this partner and the budget motel were gone. Again, Mr. Brown kept the technology and the plant.

Obviously, there was a big learning curve in this new modular building business. Mr. Brown was narrowing in on who would be an ideal partner.

His next choice would bring all this together.

Holiday Inn, the Prelude

Kemmons Wilson founded Holiday Inn in the early 1950's about the same time that Donn Corp. was started. The story goes that Mr. Wilson, who was a homebuilder, was on a family driving vacation and was disturbed that he could not find good places for his family to stay. He started franchising Holiday Inn hotels. By 1972, he was on the cover of Time Magazine, and ran a giant, successful, Fortune 500 business with 1400 hotels.

Mr. Wilson was building several hundred new hotels a year, and he also manufactured or supplied everything it took to run them from the beds and furniture to the linens. Kemmons Wilson had a well-earned reputation as a brilliant entrepreneur and creative builder of a whole industry-the quality roadside motel.

All this made Mr. Wilson and Holiday Inn (HI) a perfect match for Mr. Brown and his Modular buildings.

The Initial Holiday Inn Deal

A team of Mr. Brown's best people (including me) was sent HI's headquarters in Memphis, Tennessee. Our goal was to present our modular motel concept and negotiate a first motel project. We were told by Mr. Brown not to return home to Ohio until we had accomplished this task. There was little doubt in his mind that this first project could lead to one of the most successful partnerships in American commerce!

The Donn Team accomplished the task but only on Holiday Inn's terms. A 150-room motel would be built in our modular plant, delivered, erected and finished out by us on their site. The $1.5 million fixed price was what HI was paying for traditional construction. HI's Team was familiar with modular buildings and they were willing to do this as a test project. But they would only pay their regular, on-site built price, no extras, and no add-ons. If this initial project went well and worked out to be cost efficient with a faster completion time, then the idea of a longer-term partnership and more projects could be discussed.

All of us on Mr. Brown's Team were thrilled we got this far with a group of famously difficult HI negotiators who really held all the cards. We rushed back to report all the details to Don Brown; we knew he would be very happy!

The Slightly Modified Holiday Inn Deal

Mr. Brown was pleased with our Team's work but he told us he was going to make a slight modification to our deal. We all repeated what HI had told us: no further changes! A fixed price based on their other projects! Take it or no deal! We all expressed terrible doubts and concerns, saying that by asking for a slight change, we could be losing our one chance to work with Holiday Inn. Why were the Donn Team members so nervous?

Because most of this Donn Team's work over the prior decade had been these, on/off, less than successful, modular projects. They were worried that Holiday Inn was the last viable chance for this business venture and maybe their careers with Mr. Brown. As the, new-to-the-Company and new-to-modular buildings, financial guy, all I knew for sure was that we and various, knowledgeable partners had lost a small fortune in this business over the last several years. The problem was that we never really built the same project twice. So estimating the costs for any new project, including the one with Holiday Inn, was a crap shoot. Also the mounting modular losses and need for cash were becoming a drain on Donn's profitable ceiling business and straining our relationship with our Bank.

After hearing our concerns repeated several times, Mr. Brown told us his plan. He would meet alone, Founder to Founder, Entrepreneur to Entrepreneur, Chairman to Chairman, with Kemmons Wilson. Now the Team was even more scared. He told us to set up the meeting but did not explain his desired modification.

Two weeks later we were flying back to Memphis while Mr. Brown explained to us what he was going to request from Mr. Wilson - what his idea of a slight modification would be.

An extra $1 million dollars on our agreed deal of $1.5 million. A Slight Modification. All of the Donn Team was dumbstruck and barely able to speak. Finally, someone managed to blurt out how do you plan to ask for this slight modification? Mr. Brown told us that he would explain to Mr. Wilson the risks a small businessman like himself faces on a project like this. He would also explain his personal desire to build affordable housing for our country. He would touch on the initial false starts and losses he had incurred in this modular business. Finally, he would promise Mr. Wilson that he would get his investment back by becoming a partner in our business and by using this modular approach to build all his future hotel projects. I don't recall whether we tried to tone down Mr. Brown's request. Everyone knew Mr. Brown's mind was made up. He was going ahead with his request.

The Donn Team waited in a conference room at Holiday Inn's headquarters. Mr. Brown was alone with Kemmons Wilson in his private office for over two hours. If we had taken a vote, the bet would be we would be riding on the plane back to Ohio with no Holiday Inn project and no hope for the modular business.

Don Brown returned from his private meeting with two things. First, he excitedly showed us, the layout for a private pond and garden to be built outside his office in Ohio to match the one of his new friend, Kemmons Wilson. Second, Mr. Wilson agreed to add a $1 million to this project. He got his slight modification.

For decades I have wondered about how Mr. Brown got the extra million. It made no sense. He was by background an engineer not a salesman. But I finally decided that he was the ultimate salesman because he had such strong knowledge, passion and belief in what he was selling. He really believed in trying to create low cost housing for America and that modular units would be the answer. And he really believed that HI needed him as well.

And somehow all his passion and interest in Modular projects formed a bond with Mr. Wilson as well. One sales guy to the other. That is True Selling!

Epilogue to the Holiday Inn Project

The 150 plus room motel was the largest project we had ever tried. It also was not just a standalone motel. It was one of the first to include what HI called the Holidome concept with meeting rooms and restaurants off the totally enclosed, covered pool and play area. We tried to build as much of it as possible in our factory but many of these Holidome areas were one-off types of rooms or lobby extensions. We also had to use much more conventional construction to have this come together and look the way Holiday Inn had specified. All of these factors led to higher project costs.

When the project was complete, we had lost money on the base contract of $1.5 million. We had lost money even with the extra, slight modification add-on of $1 million. In fact we lost about an extra $1 million on top of the $2.5 million that Holiday Inn paid.

It was our first and last project with Holiday Inn.

The fishpond and garden were built outside Mr. Brown's private office in Ohio and looked great.

But when you think about it, trying to sell anyone and especially HI, a modular hotel was some kind of True Selling!

Lessons Learned From True Selling

Everyone in business and life Sells, all the time; some people are just better at it and some things are much harder to Sell.

There are ways to become a Marketing Superstar:
- You can become a boundless Promoter
- You can focus on a Specialty niche
- But it's easier to be successful if you are in a small group and far from headquarters

When coming to corporate headquarters from the field:
- Understand headquarter's limited viewpoint
- Spend a lot of time integrating yourself there
- Be prepared to adapt your views and style

As with Don Brown and Modules, if you have a strong belief and knowledge, you can Sell anything, regardless of the product or the odds.

6. Advisors

(Good, Bad and Dealing with Them)

The Mockingbirds and the Crows

The state bird of Florida is the Mockingbird. It is a medium size, 9-inch bird that eats all kinds of insects. Mockingbirds are aptly named because they can mimic over 40 different birdcalls. They can fly like a helicopter hovering in one place or dart around at seemingly impossible angles. They mate in the spring, often in bougainvillea bushes, which have thorns to protect their nests. They will also dive bomb anyone within 25 feet of that nest and aim for your head and other vital parts. In addition, they are very smart birds that recognize human troublemakers. I know this because I am on the Florida Mockingbird trouble list.

My Florida friend, Alan, and I, dressed in bike helmets and carrying a protective broom were viciously attacked one day while trying to see if we could peacefully relocate them away from the bush by our front door to a higher end neighborhood. We lost that battle but three days later a baby mockingbird left the nest and the neighborhood was safe once more. I also gained tremendous respect for these small creatures. Mockingbirds work together, using their birdcalls, to guard their nest and babies from the occasional, well-meaning retired Florida guys and from the ever-present and hungry Crows.

Crows are considered one of the most intelligent animals on earth. Like Rats, they have been on the planet forever. Like Rats, they thrive near humans.

Like Rats, Crows eat anything! A special treat is the offspring of other birds, like our friends, the Mockingbirds. Recently, I told this to a Florida friend who said, oh no, birds only eat bugs and stuff! She obviously has not been paying attention. Crows have been trained to build and use tools to get what they want. Crows have even been trained to use vending machines. My friend with the bicycle helmet and I even watched as Crows managed to unzip a bike seat bag to steal a sandwich. They even zipped it back up so no one would notice. And Crows fly in a distinct, methodical slow flapping style because they are not in a hurry. Crows, you see, are very comfortable in their own feathers.

Crows are also very social. They can imitate the human voice like parrots. They travel and hunt in flocks. Thus Crows would have been naturals in the USG Financial Workout because a flock of Crows is also called a Murder. And the way Crows attack in a group is called Mobbing. Baby Crows stay in the nest a month longer than the young hard-working Mockingbirds. Crows also grow to well over a foot, weigh over a pound, and live much longer than most other birds. And Crows know they are superior, bigger, stronger, and smarter than all other birds. They are the Wizards of the bird world.

Which brings us to our subject-Advisors. Advisors all believe they are far smarter and have better educations and backgrounds than their slow, simple clients. Advisors, like a mobbing of Crows, want to feed, (AKA collect fees), endlessly on their clients. Advisors come in groups and have their own secret language and forms of communication. How can a mere client stand a chance? By acting like the Mockingbirds. Aggressively protect your company by openly working together with your own team. Learn to move quickly like the Mockingbirds to outmaneuver the slower Crows. And remember you have what they want and crave, money for fees! Learn to manage, be in control of, and benefit from using Advisors, not the other way around.

I started my work career as an Advisor (CPA). Several of my Mentors were Advisors (Lawyers). In my corporate roles, I have hired, fired and worked with almost every type of Advisor that exists. Sometimes I worked with them by my choice and sometimes, like in a financial crisis, I had no choice of the specific advisor.

Over the years, I have even given several talks at Northwestern's Kellogg Business School on this topic. In those days, I may have sugar-coated aspects or used general examples.

But now, like the Mockingbird, I go for the head or vitals!

Lawyers

Since two of my personal career Mentors were Lawyers it makes sense to start here. Besides being trained and molded by my Mentors, I have spent a huge amount of time with Lawyers. My USG Workout lawyer friend, Eric, used to introduce me to each set of new Lawyers by stating in, his very low key way: "Brad has spent more time with Lawyers than any non-lawyer or person not convicted of a felony I have ever known." (For a while, you could add O.J. Simpson to that list of non-lawyer, non-felons who spent a lot of time with Lawyers but he has recently spent time in a Nevada prison.)

My vast experience convinces me that it's best to approach Lawyers and all the other Advisor categories the same way. First, I will list out what they, as a group, do Good and what they, as a group, do Bad. By using and trusting each group's Good you can maximize your experience. By managing or avoiding their Bad, you will make life easier and less costly. At the end of all our Advisor reviews, we will look at Rules to work more productively with them regardless of the Advisor type.

Now for some Legal Disclosures (always a must with Advisors):

1) I have friends in all these Advisor groups.
2) No Advisor was injured during the writing of this Chapter that we know of but we do not warranty that.

Lawyers: The Good
Third Party Objectivity

It sounds simple, but often it is very hard, for a Company to be objective about a subject especially a subject that is dear to their culture or history. Of all Advisors, Lawyers are about the best at being objective. This is due to the fact that a Lawyer is a Lawyer first, and a member of a law firm, second. They are true to the practice of law and the legal profession. So a Lawyer can be objective, and at times, a great Advisor.

Creditability with Boards of Directors

Many Board members, like many corporate Officers, are afraid especially when their company is dealing with a new or troubling area. At these times, Boards really do not want to hear their internal officers talk, they want to hear from an external Lawyer. During USG's Workout, the external Lawyers were critical to the Board. We could make our own recommendations along with our Banking Wizards but often the Board or a key member of the Board just had to hear from our head external Lawyer, Frank, to get his view or his agreement once we were done talking.

And, trust me on this one, as a corporate officer or even the Chairman making a pitch to the Board, you had better know ahead of time what your head external Lawyer will say on the subject, if the Board asks him. This is absolutely critical if the matter is enterprise shaping like merging your company or dealing with major litigation or bankruptcy. There are times a respected external Lawyer can have more impact on the Board than even the Chairman. Why? Directors are very worried about their possible liability if something goes wrong and often only the external Lawyer's explanation will provide comfort. Be smart, work with your Lawyer ahead of the meeting to avoid problems.

Manage and Execute Complex Activities

The training Lawyers receive allows them to deal with activities in a linear, problem solving way. They can gather, merge, sort and lay out many diverse facts. That is the reason that most physical closing meetings for a major merger/divestiture, financing, or restructuring occur at the Lawyers. By contrast,

Bankers, many of whom are lawyers as well, really do not want to deal with making all the pieces come together. It is really hard work! And the Bankers would agree the big law firms have the best in-house food to enjoy while you sit around and wait. So be glad that Lawyers like and are good at the details.

The other aspect of managing complexity is understanding that Lawyers work best with other Lawyers. Yes, there are egos and issues from time to time, but not like Bankers. When two parties have worked out all the terms, two good sets of Lawyers can go "paper the deal" and get it done. Now it's still likely that you must go through the paperwork for days to reach final agreement, but generally, that is because one of the business parties is weak or did a bad job of instructing their attorney.

Good Lawyers, when properly instructed by their clients, can even work together to get much of a deal done. This occurred when IMC Global sold its Salt business to a New York private equity firm. The two giant New York law firms, with only minor business people helping, managed to bring it all together in a very professional and cooperative way.

So that is the Good Lawyer stuff, now about the rest.

Lawyers: The Bad

Act as the Principal Negotiator

Lawyers, like Bankers, love to try to take over a negotiation. It really does not matter whether it's a sale of a business, a strategic alliance, or a financing. Do not ever let this happen! The problem is two-fold. First, most Lawyers, to put it nicely, lack a consensual personality style that helps bring people and issues together.

Lawyers are trained to be confrontational; that is who they are and it often serves you and them well. But not as the lead negotiator.

Second, most non-lawyers look at Lawyers taking over in a bad way. Either they are too smart or too rigid or too detailed or too lawyer-like. So use their skills and their tough style to help you but do not let them take over. An example was in the USG Workout. Our external Lawyer, Frank, was considered an aggressive personality who disliked many other Lawyers and most Bankers. So once in a while, we would bring Frank to a meeting with some of our Creditor Committee Wizards and just have him yell at them for a while. After one such meeting, an otherwise aggressive, young Banker Wizard asked me, very politely for once, if we could exclude Frank from the next meeting. Later that day, we even won something because of Frank!

Lead or Develop the Overall Strategy

This is related to but different from the above. Let's say you are working on a complex, first time transaction like a Strategic Alliance with an international firm. There are a million legal issues. Technology. Royalties. Treaties. Taxes. You cannot let the Lawyers lead the whole planning or strategy discussion. The strategy should be formed by the Company and led by the Company who presents it to the other party. Even the legal issues like technology need to be vetted inside your Company first to help you decide on the key issues or terms. Then a good Lawyer can help you frame it, legally.

Lawyers: The In Between (Good and Bad)

Managing Conflicts of Interests.

It used to be that Lawyers were very clear on not representing two parties in one transaction and thus they avoided a Conflict of Interest. Nowadays this has changed. Many large law firms have special practices that cater to private equity firms which like to buy anything in sight. Often their targets are part of a large public company.

These large public companies are often major corporate clients of the same law firms. The Lawyers try to deal with this by having a whole separate group who only work on deals with the private equity people versus their regular corporate group. Lawyers are also very proactive, pointing out these issues to their corporate clients who are then asked to sign a formal release allowing the conflict to occur.

An issue related to a Conflict of Interest is the use or misuse of client confidential information within the same law firm. This never really became an issue in my deals but Lawyers should think hard about how to protect client confidentiality. After all, Lawyers never want to be thought of like Bankers!

Which leads us to our next Advisor group, the much maligned and yet often not understood world of Bankers.

Bankers

Before we dive into the world of Bankers, a brief history is in order. For decades we had commercial bankers and investment bankers. Commercial bankers took in deposits, granted loans and made money on the difference. On a limited basis, they invested in government bonds and other securities. Commercial bankers looked at clients with a long term view as both their deposits and loan agreements usually had long maturities.

By contrast, Investment bankers, as stockbrokers, advised clients and charged a fee for investing in securities. They also advised ever-changing corporate clients on selling bonds, stock, or their company, also for a fee. Their outlook was far more short-term. Investment bankers also traded stocks, bonds, or anything and were much more highly leveraged with debt.

For decades, the two types of Bankers could not do each other's jobs or merge. All this changed in 1999, when Congress and President Clinton made it lawful for a commercial and investment bank to be one firm, now called a Banker. Some of us in the business world (me) and Congress think the old separate approach was better. The roles and client relationships were more clearly defined. There were fewer conflicts of interest. Now we have Bankers/Wizards who are too big to fail! And all this blurs the lines between what Bankers do good and what they do bad.

<u>Bankers: The Good</u>

Explain the Rules of the Game

In our review of USG's Financial Crisis we covered the Rules of a Workout or Restructuring. As you recall, the Bankers explained there were no rules and no secrets in Workout. But our Wizard Banker friends are actually very good at explaining the rules of whatever game you play with them. In an auction/business sale they establish a timetable, put together a book or selling prospectus for your business, then find you buyers.

In a stock or bond sale, they go through a similar process. Bankers organize a road show where you travel by private plane around the U.S. for a week telling the story they helped you put together. Hopefully, this ends with orders from investors who want to buy your stock or bonds. And if either your auction or your stock or bond sale are successful, (which means the Bankers get a huge fee), they organize the best part, the closing celebration dinner! The dinner is usually in your city at an expensive restaurant you personally would not pay to go to. But this dinner, which the Bankers pay for, has speeches, gag gifts, and a souvenir Lucite tombstone to commemorate them and the deal forever! Enjoy the celebration, your Company paid for it!

Expand Available Alternatives and Options

Everyday some company or its Board hires a Banker to "explore strategic alternatives." What this really means is that the poor company has run out of some combination of money or strategy or leadership. But they have come to the right place.

Bankers are really good at providing, for a fee, more options and alternatives than you could ever dream up.

During the USG Crisis we searched for a potential investor as we were running out of money. Our two Bankers literally divided the world based on who they knew best. Bankers have a global reach and they help companies do a hard thing: sell themselves. But USG in those days was a very hard sell. Twenty-five investor candidates later, No Deal.

But Bankers do not just find investors. You need a technology alliance, for a fee you got it! Sell, at a loss, that subsidiary they helped you buy a few years before, for a fee, you got it! Do a merger where your chairman comes out on top, for a bigger fee, you got it! Providing options and choices for Boards through their global network is the true core competence of Bankers.

But as they used to say on TV's cop show, Hill Street Blues, just be careful out there; playing or exploring fee-based options with the Bankers can be dangerous to your corporate health!

Execute Standard Financial Transactions

This may sound obvious but it is how Bankers got started, doing basic sales of stock and bonds for a small fee. Add to this, advising firms on deals and providing the financing requirements for acquisitions and divestitures, for a small fee. Today, Bankers prefer to say they advise clients on a full range of activities.

That is because the Banker's fee structure on general advising is much higher than the standard fees for issuing stock or bonds. That said, standard financial transactions are one thing Bankers do well. By contrast, the more general advising, like debt restructuring or finding a strategic partner, is much harder, but more profitable, than the bread and butter transactions that Bankers do so well.

Bankers: The Bad

Conflicts of Interest

The world of Bankers is a never-ending world of conflicts. Part of this ties into the Good concept that Bankers know everyone, everywhere in the world. That is why they are Wizards. But this also leads to conflicts. One day you can hire a Banker to defend you and the next day they show up with a new client who wants to buy you. This is how USG came to buy its Chicago neighbor, Masonite. The now-gone Salomon firm first helped Masonite fend off a hostile takeover attempt. Sometime later they came to USG with the brilliant idea of buying Masonite. USG bought it and a few years later, sold it, again with Salomon's help. That is a lot of fees and maybe a few conflicts. Which leads us to our next issue.

Confidentiality

All day long, Bankers will swear on Bibles or other religious books that they maintain Confidentiality. They will tell you this as it relates to your firm, its secrets and the outside world. They will tell you that they maintain strict Chinese walls between the various activities their firm performs. The theory and the intent are probably there, but often the practice is not. You see, even though Bankers are Wizards, they are people too. And people, everywhere, love to talk.

It's a lot like Conflicts of Interests. Because Bankers know people everywhere and may start showing them, in confidence, your secret brochure, eventually someone is going to talk. That is why it's wise and why Lawyers often recommend to make a public announcement. This is best if your plan is to sell a business or search for a merger partner as part of exploring strategic options. I have had a public company Chairman "test the waters" by having a trusted Banker just talk to one or two people about a possible deal. Within three days, some of our concerned customers and creditors were calling. It is not just Workout that has No Secrets; it's most of the world of our Wizard Bankers!

Explaining Risk

When USG went through its financial crisis, we issued a lot of junk bonds, securities that are not rated among the safest of investments. They were issued by Salomon and Goldman Sachs. A couple of years later, we were into our Workout and the bonds were selling for 25% of what the buyers paid. We obtained a list of who owned the bonds. Some were owned by large banks and insurance firms and large pension plans. OK. But somehow a private funeral home trust in a small Pennsylvania town, where Donn had a plant, owned $9 million! What did that bond salesman say to get them to buy our bonds and what was his commission?

Our federal government and various states have sued every major bank (JPMorgan/Chase, Citicorp, and Bank of America) for billions for lying about the credit worthiness of mortgages they or an acquired firm sold. Did anyone understand, yet alone explain the risks? Don't bet on it.

Management Consultants

There was a time when Consultants, like Bankers, were easier to understand. Just like commercial bankers morphed into investment bankers and vice versa, Consultants have also morphed to get more opportunities to collect fees.

Once it was possible to categorize the work of Consultants into logical areas. Strategy which was dominated by McKinsey and Booz. Operations with Accenture on systems, CSC on process engineering and A.D. Little on process manufacturing. But nowadays some of the largest Consulting firms are the accounting firms and former manufacturing giants like HP or IBM.

We have also witnessed an explosion in organizational or culture consulting. Once, only retired human resource people would venture there, but now everyone is willing to help clients with their soft issues like crisis management, downsizing and, of course, coaching for individuals or whole teams.

Like the Bankers, Consultants are expanding their footprint (a consultant's word), into all kinds of emerging or trendy new areas. They would say that this better serves the ever-changing needs of their clients. I would say it occurs to get more shots at more fees from those same organizations.

Still, Management Consultants do some things Good and some things Bad. The Good endure. Sadly the Bad items have not changed much over time even though the Consultants have!

As always, we will begin with The Good.

Management Consultants: The Good

Provide a Framework.

Consultants' business is the world of presentations. They have the latest graphics, tools, multimedia charts and videos. They are also constantly repackaging or relabeling their own business. In addition, they have full time professionals in all the technical aspects of presentations. So if your project is strategy their firm invented and published in the Harvard Business Review (or their own quarterly magazine) the latest framework for this area. If it's operations or systems, one of their senior people just published a whole book that blankets your issue.

And if it's organizational, they did a study for President Obama's initial transition team or, if you are McKinsey, several of your top people were hired to work in the White House. And yes, they really do all these things and they do them really well.

In fact, their Frameworks are so good that without even studying your firm from the inside, they can come to your executive team retreat, as CSC once did to USG, and in a half hour presentation of their latest theory about what traits makes companies excel, get your somewhat stodgy staff arguing all evening about what they are really good at!

So let them help you create a Framework for your project.

Provide Comfort and Creditability.

All Advisors should be able to provide a level of comfort to senior management or the Chairman or owner who hired them. In public companies this is extremely important, whether it should be or not. Consultants are the best at providing comfort.

When our Donn grid business was acquired and combined with the USG's tile business, USG hired an industrial psychology firm to interview all our senior people. They reported to us how different we were and how hard it would be to combine the groups. I thought it was accurate, but again wondered, what value USG or its Board obtained from the report since it was completed after the merger. Still, Boards love Consultants.

When Donn was being sold to USG we tried to benefit from this by hiring McKinsey to work for us. McKinsey helped us prepare a selling presentation for USG that was quite good. This was how Donn tried to provide comfort to USG's management and Board. The old adage is true-a Board of Directors will tend to believe an opinion from an outside Consultant, even if it is the same opinion expressed by their own people. As Star Trek's Mr. Spock would say, "It is not logical, but it is often true." So understand and use Consultants for what you want rather than being used by them!

Facilitate a Change Process.

If you need to make a significant change that involves operations or staff management, it will be more quickly and easily accepted if it comes from Consultants versus your own people. This makes no sense but it is nevertheless true. When USG wanted to combine all 25 Gypsum and Ceilings business customer order centers into one location, we used Accenture to help. Since we were essentially closing down all 25 existing order centers and putting hundreds of people out of work, Accenture provided a blanket of cover and respectability for the whole project. And they crafted the perfect rationale; we could save millions, put in a state of the art computer system, and make life easier for our customers all at the same time!

Accenture also provided a perfect buffer between the various elements that had to work together: the corporate systems group, the Gypsum internal and external sales group and the Ceiling internal and external sales group. With a lot of early meetings and consensus building sessions, the team I headed was able to pull this off, on time and within the tens of millions of dollars budget. So projects involving facilitating change are a perfect use of Consultants. You must manage them but this is an area where they can really earn their fee.

Management Consultants: The Bad
Recommend a Specific Tactic

Just as Consultants are great on Frameworks, they are weak on the movement from broad strategy to detailed implementation steps. The problem they often run into is this: the Client's culture or systems just do not mix with their brilliant theory.

And culture, especially, is very hard to overcome. Sometimes the Consultants just let their analysis get the better of them. After McKinsey advised Donn on its sale to USG, they were hired by USG. The project was to study the marketing options for Donn grid and USG's APCO tile. McKinsey interviewed dozens of separate and joint ceiling distributors and contractors to get their opinions. Almost all the customers said it would be best to keep the sales and marketing of ceiling grid and tile separate. In the world of construction, these two products need to arrive and be installed almost simultaneously on the construction job site. This is true whether one company owns both products or not. Our customers worried about losing their influence over pricing if the tile and grid were sold as a package. McKinsey, in one of its few bad suggestions, said we should keep the products separate. We combined them instead; it was the right and successful move. Company 1, Consultants 0.

Transfer Learning to the Client

This is one of my main complaints with Consultants who tend to guard their processes and tools as if they were some secret. For example, Consultants rarely like to have company people on their team and if they do, they prefer low level people who are no threat to their secrets. Or they will let one of your people assist in the interviewing or data gathering but not with recommendations. This approach is shortsighted especially since what Consultants are selling is the next great framework or concept not the one they already used on you. Part of this may relate to a theory we discussed earlier, that many Advisors truly believe that all Clients are not smart enough to comprehend their Wizard-like skills.

There has been some movement away from this rigid approach. At USG Interiors, we used Tom Kuczmarski's Innovation firm, whose main objective was to help teach us how to identify and bring new products to market. Everyone thought this Consultant project was well worth the fee. Advisors could improve their image and make more fees if they learn to share!

Understanding the Client's Culture

Consultants, like most Advisors, focus on who hired them and that is it. Usually this is the Chairman or the Board or the President of a business. This top focus prevents the Consultants from fully understanding the company's unique culture. Instead Consultants really need to focus more on the internal teams and their issues and obstacles not just on the senior person who hired them. I have found this especially troubling in so-called organization or culture studies headed by Human Resources.

Often Human Resources provides a brief, sanitized summary of the findings, which usually include massive contradictions or inconsistencies. But everyone knows the Chairman or the Board was given something else. This does not create trust or team building even if it does help some H.R. person's job security.

So the Advice to the Consultants is, if you really want to be re-hired, you should consider who might be making future decisions and try to take the bias out of your reports.

Common Issues with Advisors

Regardless of what category of Advisors we listed, everyone has the same, common issues with them:

Training and Development: This is a decades old issue. You or your team train the Advisor in your company/industry and within a month they are working for your competitors telling them what experts they are.

Repackaging Expertise: This occurs two ways. First, every Advisor takes the same common business cycle or procedure and renames it to create a new service within their brand. So at one firm they call it reengineering, at another value or supply chain and so on... Second, is how the same individual Advisor Wizard reappears, first as an expert in issuing securities, then restructuring, then global alliances and so on.

<u>Conflict with Client Goals:</u> Companies want to do their projects fast, at low cost, and with no publicity. Advisors want to stretch out the work and the fees and gain fame or at least publish the success they had with you.

<u>Confidentiality</u>: Do we need to warn you again?

<u>Greed and Fees:</u> You got this one by now!

Rules to Deal with Advisors

Despite all this, you and your business will hire Advisors, and if you are lucky (or unlucky) probably dozens of them in the course of a career. So what are some things you should do to minimize your pain and expense and enhance the Advisor's value?

<u>Fee Negotiations</u>

First, avoid Chairman or Owner involvement. Advisors love dealing at the top! You do not want this to occur as it will cost you more or you will pick the wrong Advisor. Or worse yet, pick the wrong project or scope. Smart Chairmen/Owners stay out.

Second, hold Beauty Contests (Advisor's term for a presentation) then have a vote. Advisors bring everyone who looks or sounds good to these meetings. See two or three groups, then vote in private.

Third, have private, pre-signing follow-up meetings. Once you have chosen a firm, but before you hire them, you need one or two of your team to meet them in person. And tell them you only want to meet those who will actually be doing the work. You do not need the big title or resumes, you need to decide if you like and can work with the specific individuals. It is amazing those they show vs. the real workers.

Fourth, Clarify Scope. Avoid being a test case. Scope of a project is critical. Sometimes it's easy, like selling a business. But often operations and systems projects need a very clear, narrow scope. Also avoid leading or bleeding edge projects. Do not be a beta test case unless you are desperate or pay a very, very, very low fee to do it.

Fifth, Place your own people on the project. And volunteer only very good, high potential people. It's not possible on every project. This can help lower fees and your team can learn a lot.

Retain Control of your Transaction or Project

Management is in charge not the Advisors. After all, You are paying their fees! It kills me how lazy or timid people get bullied around by their Advisors. Be a tough Mockingbird! You have what the Crows want, a fee! Make them earn it!

Protect Your Company's Interests

Put a tight Confidentiality Agreement in place with your Advisor. They will fight and moan but you need at least 2 years protection; longer for securities deals.

Play to the Advisor's Strength

Remember the Good things we covered for each type of Advisor like explaining rules, giving your Board comfort, and executing transactions. But use the Good with care. Why? With many strengths, come the Bad flip sides: lack of confidentiality or conflicts of interests. All Advisors have Good and Bad issues that you need to manage to prevent things getting Ugly.

Dealing with Complexity

We spoke about this in the USG Financial Crisis but it is worth repeating. Almost all the many, major projects you will hire Advisors for are very complex. So learn their rules well but also verify with an outside party that the rules your Advisor is telling you are accurate. And remember The Rule of Three, if something three-peats in your project from the inside or outside, listen.

Communicate, Communicate Internally

This is the last but maybe the most important Rule for dealing with Advisors. Create detailed project schedules, use daily phone trees with your team, and have weekly meetings with your Advisors as to status, scope, fees and monthly meetings with senior management, as well as with your Board or owner. Be like the agile Mockingbirds dealing with those powerful Crows.

GOOD LUCK! And learn to live with Advisors!

Lessons Learned from Advisors

To Benefit and Survive with your Advisors/Crows, learn from the Mockingbird Company Team: be quick, work together seamlessly, and communicate! The Company should be in control, it pays the fees!

Lawyers as Advisors are Good at:
- Bringing third party objectivity
- Providing creditability with Boards/Owners
- Managing and executing complex deals

Lawyers as Advisors are Bad at:
- Acting as the head negotiator
- Creating the overall strategy

Bankers as Advisors are Good at:
- Explaining the rules of the game
- Expanding your alternatives and options
- Executing standard financial transactions

Bankers are Bad at:
- Avoiding conflicts of interest
- Maintaining confidentiality
- Explaining risks

Management Consultants are Good at:

- Providing a framework or packaging issues
- Giving comfort and creditability to issues
- Facilitating a change process

Management Consultants are Bad at:

- Recommending a specific tactic
- Transferring learning to their clients
- Understanding a company's culture

Common Issues with All Advisors:

- Training their ever-changing, youthful staff
- Constantly repackaging their framework and expertise
- Having goals that conflict with their clients: Fees vs. cost; privacy vs. fame
- Maintaining and safeguarding confidentiality
- Focusing on fees and greed, as Advisors are Wizards!

Rules for Dealing with Advisors:

- Manage the fee negotiation process
- Control your project - you pay the fees!
- Protect your company's interests/confidentiality
- Play to the Advisor's strengths (Good vs. Bad)
- Learn to deal with project complexity
- Communicate, communicate within your client team

7. Human Resources

(Inhuman Resources, the Last C Suite)

Picking up after the Elephant

Human Resource (HR) professionals have been called many things. Many not complimentary or kind. In the cartoon, Dilbert, HR is the evil Catbert. Some of my old associates called them Inhuman Resources.

In recent decades, the movement to massive downsizings and layoffs have not helped HR's public relations image. But it has increased their power.

Historically, Human Resources was not a major position or even a Board appointed role. Titles like President, Treasurer and Secretary are required by most state laws for public, private, and even not-for-profit groups. President evolved to CEO or COO. Treasurer to CFO. But companies used to just have a Personnel manager. That has all changed.

News Flash! Consulting giant IBM has a free newsletter for C Suite officers. In these ads IBM lists CEOs, COOs, CFOS, CIO (information) and CHROs, as their targeted C Suite officers, officers to whom they want to provide free wisdom (and later receive $$$$ consulting fees).

At first I thought this last one, CHRO, was a typo or a food offering at Chipotle. So I called my recently retired, Senior HR officer friend, Gary.

He corrected me, in his best coaching manner. This is indeed, a new title, Chief HR Officer and he said at his last job he had this new title. When I asked if this was a joke, he kindly, but sternly said no, then changed the subject to something less controversial, like the death of one of our retired friends.

Apparently, I concluded, some group of HR people had come up with this as an improvement on Chief Administrative Officer (CAO) since it was a way to pay themselves more money and not always be the lowest paid officer on the corporate totem pole. The CAO title always amused me since it meant the HR people also were in charge of the headquarters building or the cafeteria or at least, the cleaning company. Since most companies with these kinds of titles had real estate people and no shortage of lawyers and accountants, I have never understood why the building needed watching by a CAO or anyone else; it does not move around much or get itself into trouble like those frisky human employees often do.

But this leads to my theory of how the onetime, humble personnel manager became the high paid, multi-titled C level corporate officer.

The Theory of Misplaced or Forfeited Power

To illustrate this, let's revisit our old friend, the King, and his brother, the Wizard. In the early days of his reign, the King, enjoyed doing all the kingly duties himself. If he needed a new general or a court jester, he would interview and hire one. If he sought a new wife or concubine, he would personally throw himself into the search. If someone in the kingdom broke his laws, he, their King, would hear their case and pass judgment on them, including at times, the death sentence. After all, this was a critical part of the King's job description.

Then one day, the King got tired or lazy or distracted. Maybe his horses or hunting or new wives were taking all his time. And that day he asked his younger brother, the Wizard, to do a task that before, only he, the King, would do. It could be as simple as hiring a new juggling act or as unpleasant as passing sentence to execute an old friend. Presto! The Wizard was now in charge! And if the Wizard was clever, we also know he will gradually take over more and more of his King brother's duties. The Wizard will claim that he just wants to relieve his King of the burden; let the King do more hunting, ride his horses more, or nowadays, to play more golf!

Suddenly, the Wizard is doing almost all of the King's duties, especially the mundane or nasty ones. The Wizard is like the guy in the circus parade who follows the elephants with a giant shovel to clean up their messes. But he is cleaning up the King's messes. The Wizard then tells the King he needs a junior wizard, or worse, a few interns. And the Wizard now wants an additional title like CEG, Chief Execution Guy. He hires the new generals and other members of the court and convinces them all that He, the Wizard, is the key to their future. Since, as CEG, he is now in charge of executions, his words have special meaning. Soon the Wizard truly is the power behind the throne but it is because the King has misplaced or forfeited his own power. And, heaven help us, if the King becomes ill or dies, then the Wizard alone will bestow the crown on the next King who will be beholding to the Wizard forever!

This is how Human Resource in many large companies got their superhuman powers. Some CEO got tired or lazy, so he let HR do it. It took time; it was messy; HR did not mind, they seemed to like the work. With the rise in recent years of corporate downsizings, sexual harassment, discrimination and wrongful dismissal suits, HR quickly and quietly, rose from their non-titled Personnel role up to the Officer's C Suite.

Now an interesting phenomenon occurs to the person who is following the elephant and cleaning up the mess. Or to the person who does all the nasty company tasks like firing longtime employees. That person, often, becomes uncaring or cold-hearted or insensitive to the people and their issues. It's like in the medical profession, you cannot save everyone and if you let each death get to you personally, you will not survive physically or mentally. So, by the time you become a senior Human Resource person, you may have lost some of your own humanity. Hence, the image of Inhuman Resources. It is like our other story of "It's Only Business, not Personal." The HR group has to be callous or hard-nosed in many of their activities and yet most of them would tell you this is only their required business persona not their real, kind and sensitive, personal self.

Let's look at some Good and Bad HR examples from small, private companies and large, public ones.

Human Resources at Donn Corporation

There were NO Human Resource professionals at Donn

AND

ALL the Donn managers were H.R. professionals

Both statements were true. And, as with almost everything at Donn, it all started with its founder/owner Don Brown.

Hiring at Donn

For most of the thirty years Mr. Brown owned Donn, he would try to personally interview all the new office hires.

Mr. Brown told me some of his secret techniques for screening people. The most important was to watch them from his office window as they walked back to their car in the parking lot after his interview. In an interview, people sat up straight and tried to project an eager, go get them image. But, as they walked back to their car, what did Mr. Brown see? Did they slump over, did their feet drag or were they still straight and tall?

Before I was hired at Donn, I was interviewed by Mr. Brown, who I had only briefly met when I was an outside auditor. I was not sure what to expect. We talked about family and that my son was about the age to join the YMCA's Indian Guides which Mr. Brown and his sons really enjoyed. We also discovered we both owned a Shetland Sheep dog. That was my interview. No questions about my education or, at age 26, my work experience. And certainly no financial questions, which I would learn later were never his focus. What I did take away from this experience was that it is more important to learn about the real person through relaxed dialogue. Quality people = quality workers.

The best lesson was that Mr. Brown would always say he was not a good manager, therefore he was careful to hire only really good managers. Generally he made excellent choices. That is what really great leaders do. Don Brown was ahead of his time.

Salary Negotiations at Donn

I hired numerous people, in finance and operating roles for Donn's affiliated businesses like module buildings or our boat and aviation group. I did this by personally researching the jobs and being flexible in what we offered to get the right individuals. Sometimes this was done with search firms, sometimes by networking and sometimes by placing ads in the Wall Street Journal. When you do the work yourself you know as much about the job description and the appropriate pay as the people you are trying to hire and certainly more than most HR people.

Donn's Annual Reviews

Don Brown believed that all salaried employees should have an annual review that was documented in a signed Compensation book. What was interesting, for its day, was that the book included all of the employee's costs to Donn. Your salary, any bonuses, auto and travel if applicable, health insurance, social security. Again, this was long before computerized employee benefit statements from consulting firms. Each book took every manager time to manually put together. But by the annual review meeting, the manager actually knew what the book said.

Donn's Clothing Allowance

Perhaps one of Don Brown's more unique reward programs was the Clothing Allowance. All salespeople, managers and the top administrative assistants were reimbursed up to $1,000 per year (in today's dollars) for business attire-suits, shoes and ties.

Sport coats, shirts and most of today's business casual clothing were not covered. That amount could get you two suits with ties. Here again, Mr. Brown's theory was simple. He wanted his people to look professional and stand out, even when it was a very small company. And that meant in the office or while traveling or dining on company business. He also believed that if he helped you get a business wardrobe going, you might spend some of your own money to expand it. Don Brown would not like today's business casual, yet alone blue jean Fridays.

$50,000 of Christmas Gifts

Don Brown started giving Christmas gifts to children of his office and plant workers at his initial Ohio location. By the time of the Donn sale to USG, we were shipping gifts to every employee's child anywhere in the Donn world. This included Canada, Europe, New Zealand and even South Africa. The rules were simple. You had to be a full-time employee for at least one year. The children had to be ages 2 to 12. That was it.

The Christmas gift process started in the fall. Letters were sent to the head Donn managers at all the locations to furnish the names, ages, and sex of each qualified child. A large Cleveland department store, today it would be Macy's, brought over several sample toys for boys and girls for each age group. Here again, Mr. Brown had rules. No weapons or war toys. Today that would eliminate a lot. The sample gifts would be spread out in Mr. Brown's office for a couple weeks and he and his Assistant, Jane, would make the choices, again by boy/girl and age group. The appropriate quantities would be ordered and shipped to the Donn Westlake plant.

Jane would ask for volunteers to personally hand wrap the toys. Every wrapped toy was sent to the various worldwide plants and given to the employee to take home in time for Christmas. Each toy was accompanied with a note to the parents from Mr. Brown. The note explained that he was enclosing a self-addressed, stamped return envelope, in case the child wanted to write him a thank you note. It was further explained that the thank you was not a requirement, but if a child did write to Mr. Brown, he would not only personally read each note, he would write the child a note thanking them for their thank you. I do believe he or Jane read every thank you note that came in.

To this day the whole process still seems massive. How did we get international postage for the return envelopes? How much did it cost to ship all the toys? The last year before the sale of the Company, the bill from the department store alone was around $50,000, 25 years ago! This did not count all the time and expense to hand wrap, ship and include the stamped return envelopes or Mr. Brown's follow-up thank you to the thank you.

What I do know is that you can ask my son, Mike, now a father himself, about the Donn Christmas gifts. Mike remembers the gifts and that they were cool. He remembers writing the thank you notes. He would also tell you that the gifts somehow created a connection for him to my workplace and to its owner, Mr. Brown. It was like Mr. Brown was investing something in him. And isn't that what Mr. Brown hoped the kids would recall?

So Donn had some unique human resource practices and some special rewards and incentives, which had nothing to do with building products. Donn plants were also almost 100% nonunion and Donn sales doubled every three years. And the Donn employees and their families somehow felt special and a part of it. My son, Mike, and I certainly did.

Today many large firms have little of this personal touch.

Human Resources at USG Corporation
Problem, Your Salary is 129% of Par!

This is what I was told by the USG HR group after I was named to head up the financial team for the newly formed USG Interiors. I was told this was not good, since the guidelines for salaries stated you should be at 80-120% of some salary par. I was further told that either I would not get a pay increase for years or I had to hope I would somehow be promoted often and quickly to avoid being lost forever at 129% of par purgatory!

A little background - When Donn was acquired, it was combined with several other large USG units to form USG

Interiors. The senior Donn managers were guaranteed their current salaries for 3 years. Donn sales became about one half of USG Interiors sales that became about one fifth of all of USG sales. In my humble view, this made my job much bigger and more important. But somehow the HR group decided that this position would be titled and paid like all their other business units, Vice President-Financial Administration. Not CFO or Controller or Treasurer of USG Interiors. I was also told that USG had all these Corporate groups that would help do some of my former duties; help from Corporate being a very old oxymoron.

The title also did not reflect the fact that this new Interiors unit had to combine 20+ businesses that came from three different companies and had no common anything-billing, chart of accounts, systems, nothing. And somehow the title ignored the fact that there were still a dozen Donn international operations of which I was titled Treasurer. I learned over time that I knew more about the new job's real responsibilities than any of the USG HR people who were assigning my title and salary range.

So what do you do when you are doomed at 129% of par and forced to take a meaningless title? Ignore it as foolishness and put your energies to work in the new role. For me, there was a lot to do pulling the new Interiors together- managerially, culturally, systems-wise and financially. Unfortunately, in large companies, this type of inflexible job and pay scales often prevents someone from taking a new role that could be great for their career. Human Resource people can be flexible and need to apply this flexibility to encourage, not discourage, moves especially into a very new or different business.

And yes, I did get promoted a lot, in a short period, so the 129% of par never mattered!

You Want to Fire the Pregnant Controller?

A couple years after forming USG Interiors, USG Corporation plunged into its Financial Crisis. Each business group had to make headcount reductions. We had two smaller Interiors businesses, Walls and Floors, which had been shrinking not growing. We decided to collapse the two business groups into one. Each had a President, a Controller and a small staff; one group would be terminated. The Wall business was by far the smallest and also had the worst financial results. It also was located in Chicago at our headquarters, so this was personal.

We decided that the Wall group Controller-Judy's job would be eliminated. She was a very hard working, bright young lady. Judy had started with USG, right out of school, and had been promoted several times before this role. She was a natural networker and an officer in a professional business organization. Judy was also expecting and about to go on maternity leave.

I met with the Interiors' HR guy, my friend Gary, and told him I wanted to talk to Judy before she went on maternity leave. This way she would have a chance to start some internal networking. Then, when she came back from her leave she would still have time to pursue opportunities before she was terminated. Normally calm Gary, lost it! He said we could not tell her until after the maternity leave, because we did not want her upset! I said she is very smart and knows we are combining the two businesses. Besides she was a real pro who could handle this news, and she would appreciate the early notice so she could start a job search. Gary was in shock. I then suggested I would handle this myself.

Judy did take the news in stride. She tried to find another role but that was not possible. After she had the baby, she told me that she and her husband had decided to use this as an opportunity to make their dream move to Florida. We rearranged her timetable and with a nice severance, they were off. I was a job reference for her for the next decade and she did very well. She always told me that she appreciated the way she was treated.

I only wanted an Aquarium!

After we completed USG Corporation's Financial Crisis, Human Resources notified me that the Board of Directors promoted me from Vice President/CFO to Senior V.P./CFO. With this promotion, I was also told I qualified for a country club. Many people would have jumped for joy.

My personal belief was that, except in very few cases, like a Senior Sales VP or Chairmen/Presidents, country clubs are a huge waste of money. The initiation fees for most Chicago area clubs could reach $100,000+. The monthly minimum dues were also high. And the value the corporation received for all this? Zero.

So I respectfully declined the country club, a rare event.

About the same time, USG had just moved into a new downtown Chicago headquarters. A nice young lady, Dixie, from USG's Office Services group, had helped layout my new office and came by to see if it was working for me. She innocently asked if there was anything else that would make my new, large office more personal. I said that I had always wanted an Aquarium. I knew there was a cost to install and maintain one but I jokingly said that I had turned down a country club, so this was cheap.

Dixie said she would investigate this for me. At this point it had not occurred to me that my request would become a big deal. But I had forgotten a key fact. Office Services reported to HR as part of managing the pesky building in that CAO title.

A couple of days later, USG's Senior VP of HR/CAO came to my new office from his new office twenty feet away. He gently shut my new office door and still standing, kindly said to me, "You cannot have an aquarium."

I had honestly already forgotten my aquarium idea.

Always interested in how HR worked, asked "Why not?"

He said, "We know you would do this tastefully and low key, but the next person would ask for a larger one and then the next person an even larger, wall sized unit."

As often with HR, I was speechless, but managed to blurt out "Really?" I did not expect a response but instead was more amazed, when he said, "Yes, in fact it could get worse. Someone could want a terrarium with lizards and snakes; think of the insurance risk!"

Obviously I dropped the Aquarium suggestion like a hot giant iguana. And I never knew if he really meant any of that stuff. So sometimes rewards can look very different to the person desiring them versus the person who grants them. That's why, I never had an office aquarium or a country club.

News Update! Several years ago, USG's Board, in the midst of another terrible housing market, eliminated all country clubs from their executive perks. I would have enjoyed being at that Board Meeting and might have offered the following advice.

Maybe you should look at aquariums. Restful. Cheap.

Before We Promote You, We Need to Shrink You!

You may recall that right at the start of the USG Financial Crisis, USG's Senior Management changed. At this time, my friend and USG boss, Gene, came to me and said I was on a short list for one of the top financial jobs. But, and this really was a BUT, since I was still new (2 years) at USG and had never visited the Company's industrial psychologist, I needed to do so and be officially shrunk. I reminded Gene that I had worked for him or the retiring CFO these last two years and asked if that provided them with enough firsthand knowledge about me.

Gene gave me one of his playful smiles and said it was all part of the game at USG. Everyone had to get shrunk!

He also told me another important truth. Some people, had already been shrunk and had to do it again. He further explained that being shrunk twice was ok, but you really wanted to avoid the third time. He ended with; I may even find it interesting.

The USG industrial psychologist was not in headquarters, probably for his personal safety. He was also not an employee of USG but an outside Advisor. He reported to, whom else, the Senior HR Vice President/CAO who organized my visit and explained to me as only HR people can the importance of this to my career, and how this process was a powerful tool at USG for promotions and determining high potential people. Yada, Yada, Yada.

And, since it was to be my first shrinking, I should show up at 9am and plan to be there most of the day including lunch with the Doctor. None of this made the visit sound enjoyable.

I tried to arrive at the Doctor's office exactly at 9am, concerned that early or late could lead to more shrinking. The first half-day was spent doing personality and career assessment type tests. Some had a time limit; some did not.

Some Personality Questions were easy to answer but some seemed tricky or filled with hidden meanings. And for each of these and a thousand more you had to circle your reaction. These are real questions. (I couldn't make this stuff up!)

- I often eat myself sick
- I have no sympathy for panhandlers
- I would rather be known as merciful than just
- I often get disgusted with people I work with (HR?)
- I am easily frightened (no, not by HR people)

The Career/Leisure Questions were equally curious.

- Career choices included forester and pilot
- Leisure activities ranged from bread making to bonsai gardening or shooting guns.

Then it was time for the one-on-one lunch with the Doctor. He drove us to his local, private country club. Now a major decision had to be made. What do you order for lunch? Is tuna too soft an item? Pasta, too loosely structured?

The lunch overall was mostly low-key chitchat perhaps because it was the intermezzo before the afternoon's big finale.

The Doctor and I spent the rest of the day together. First, we used wooden blocks to build a structure with his trusty time watch recording the progress. Then we looked at the famous inkblots. I had been warned by an older USG friend not to describe any inkblot as a part of the male or female anatomy and to avoid too many warlike or devil symbols. So I saw a lot of peaceful, nature scenes that day. Then came a surprise.

The Doctor asked me to tell him my life story. Talking I knew I could do. He further explained, I should take my time, and focus on major events or situations that were important to me. OK, sounds great. Then the Doctor mentioned an unexpected wrinkle. While I am talking, he will throw in unrelated questions and I have to give him an immediate response. Hm. Although there may have been many questions, we will focus on the three questions, which occurred as I was telling of the saddest times of my life.

Brad: my grandfather dies when I am 13

1. Doctor: Who was first to circumnavigate the globe?

Brad: Magellan

Brad: my grandmother dies when I am 15

2. Doctor: How many miles from New York to Paris?

Brad: 3600 miles

Brad: my father dies when I am 26

3. Doctor: Who wrote Faust?

Brad: Goethe

Magellan I thought everyone should know. The flight I had done a lot including on the Concorde. Goethe and Faust, I just knew.

The Doctor has made notes during all of my story and, of course, during the questions and answers. He now tells me we are done and asks if I need any directions. I said no I live in downtown Chicago. He asks where? I say 1300 North. He asks the name of my Street? I say Goethe, he wrote Faust. The Doctor flips back in his notes and crosses out my correct answer!

Well, with or without the Doctor's help, I was named USG's Chief Financial Officer. But a few years later, someone replaced my old boss, Gene, as Chairman. I have often imagined that if the Doctor had not crossed out my Goethe answer, would I have been named Chairman?

An Aside 1: Faust is the story of a scholar who sells his soul to the Devil for fame and fortune. Change a couple names and I wrote about Faust somewhere in all this.

An Aside 2: An unnamed USG friend took the same test. That night at dinner he tells his wife and kids about it. Each time he says a question, his bright 5th grade son quickly answers. My friend looks up the questions because his son's answers were almost all different from those he gave. The son's answers are 100% Right. My friend mentions this later to someone who knows Jeff Foxworthy and the old TV Show, "Are You Smarter than a 5th Grader" was born! Industrial Psychologists everywhere are upset!

The Champion of Diversity

One day my HR friend, Gary, called with a new idea. USG was starting a Diversity program to help women and minorities advance in the company. Historically, most of USG's senior people were Irish men, and Italians were considered a minority. At the time, Diversity in the overall construction industry, at any level, was limited. So this seemed like a really good HR idea. I asked, Gary, what was the plan?

The Plan was to form a committee of interested women and minorities. But Senior Management, meaning Human Resources, thought we needed a Champion of Diversity. This should be a Senior Management person who could relate to the younger committee. Finding such a senior officer, in many large companies, could a problem. But Gary and HR had a Plan.

It had been suggested (corporate talk for HR suggested), that I be the first Champion of Diversity. I realized that this was a desperation move as I was the new, younger, senior officer from the outside. It was further suggested that I could work well with the young Diversity committee. And we did.

The Diversity committee worked really hard at this and well before other large firms, USG had a number of programs in place. These included work from home days, adoption legal cost assistance and a nursing room.

It really was a good HR idea!

Cross Company Mentoring for Women

Another good idea USG's HR group had was to sign up with a not-for-profit professional development program for high potential women managers. There are several of these in the country now but in the early 1990's this was still novel. USG made a donation, and then contributed one Senior Executive, as a mentor, and one woman Manager or Director, to be mentored by someone from another organization. The program consisted of one-to-one mentoring meetings, business education seminars and an ongoing peer network.

By now you can guess who was recommended to be USG's first Senior Executive Mentor, me. The mentor's role was to help steer the mentoring relationship and provide some level of wisdom and guidance to a younger woman manager. The formal program lasted one year and covered whatever was critical to develop or advance the individual's career.

I did this for a number of years and developed some great relationships with a number of very bright and truly high potential woman managers. And I still keep up with a couple of them years later.

Another good HR idea.

Lessons Learned from Human Resources

Overall

- Real Manager/Leaders should do most of their own people duties, not defer to HR
- Personnel became an HR Officer in part due to misplaced or forfeited power from others
- Picking up after the Elephant and doing all the dirty jobs can often make someone inhuman

Smaller, private firms

- Often everyone becomes, by necessity, an HR professional
- Can afford to be more creative and innovative in dealing with people issues and incentives
- Simple rewards like holiday gifts for kids win loyalty

Large, public companies

- Can become rigid with salary guidelines, hiring practices and understanding rewards
- Should have management evaluate staff themselves and not rely on psychologists or other outside consultants
- Can introduce innovative people programs like Diversity or Mentoring with the right leaders
- Should be upfront and honest even with a pregnant Controller, or any soon to be terminated employee, which is the best and only way to be and it's truly appreciated

A small or large firm's image is always worth considering something like a clothing allowance vs. blue jean Fridays (California may be the exception).

If asked to be shrunk, try to be absent that day!

Aquariums should be considered as rewards due to their Zen value versus golf country clubs.

In Conclusion:
- The junior C Suite HR group should not be solely in charge of employment and promotion practices or incentives. All of senior management should be involved.
- Human Resource people need to practice what they often preach, showing restraint and concern with their new powers to keep the Human-versus-Inhuman title.
- The old concept of Servant Leadership should be the standard for HR people. Only, if and after they serve well, can they lead.

8. International Business
(Chile, a Country not a Food)

An International State of Mind

For those of us who are lucky enough to be born, live and work in the United States, thinking globally or Internationally does not come easy. There are a number of reasons for this. The U.S. is one of the largest, most populated and, in the last 100 years, most dominating economic country in the world.

We can name Britain's William and Kate in a photo but not that woman who currently runs Germany. When offered a globe we would have better chance shooting it through a basketball hoop than finding the Philippines or Iceland. The bulk of our news is local and national. We often learn about the outside world because of the media's coverage of natural disasters like Japan's earthquake and tsunami or the Olympics every 4 years.

In addition, we are blessed with so many great travel choices in the U.S. that travel elsewhere is not a priority. Our total use of English, the lack of serious second language studies, and our unwillingness to move to metrics does not help us feel comfortable in the non-American world.

Having spent a lot of time with Europeans and Asians I have learned that they view all this much differently. Most European countries mandate serious language studies. Schools in Sweden require English through high school. Young people in Europe and Asia all recognize our Presidents. Our athletes like LeBron James are known everywhere. Families vacation in other counties. Youth look for any excuse to travel to the U.S.

So how do U.S. business people and companies develop an International state of mind? Let's look at some examples.

Donn's Approach to International

In the case of Donn, its founder and owner had an International state of mind. Don Brown was born in Canada, and had served in WWII in Europe. So not long after the Donn business was started in Ohio, he started looking to expand abroad.

The key to International growth, Don Brown believed, was people. And to his way of thinking, you needed local people, on the ground that spoke the language, not expatriate Americans. You also needed experienced local people who understood your industry; not someone who needed training. You needed self-starting people, people he could motivate with money, so they would be successful. Time, which is always critical in business, is even more critical when you expand globally. So Mr. Brown found experienced, local, self-starting, and money motivated people. And if they got a new global start-up profitable within two years everyone made a lot of money. If not, both the business and the local Donn people were gone.

Once Don Brown found the right people, his preferred development and growth pattern for these International businesses was usually the same. Initially, we would export product from the U.S. We would then establish a legal branch operation, which allowed one of our profitable businesses to deduct the initial startup costs. Once the sales volumes built up, we would lease a small plant and ship old equipment to begin local production and create a separate corporate subsidiary.

The pace of International expansion at Donn was quite rapid. In less than a decade from the U.S. start, a Canadian business was formed. Europe started just a few years after Canada.

And then there were joint venture companies in South Africa and New Zealand/Australia. Asia followed with Malaysia and then Taiwan.

By the time of Donn's sale to USG Corporation and within thirty years of its U.S. founding, International sales accounted for 25% of Donn's total sales and were growing faster than the domestic market.

Let's look at some of Donn's International successes and failures and include some USG Corporation examples as well.

Branco, Donn Europe and Other People's Money

You may remember Branco as the elusive, master salesman and diner in Lunches and Dinners.

Branco had worked for the building giant, Armstrong, for a number of years before Don Brown hired him. He was living in Germany, Europe's largest economy, so that is where Donn Europe started. After a year of importing product from the U.S., Donn Germany began local manufacturing, with old equipment and tooling and a Technical Assistance agreement with the U.S. Within two years sales exceeded $500,000 ($2 million today) which generated a profit and no need for further U.S. funding.

Within two more years, Branco went to France and hired Chris from a ceiling competitor. Within three years, Donn France became a subsidiary of Donn Germany and began their own local manufacturing with the help of a French government development grant. With little help, France had profits in their first year.

About the same time, Branco hired Brian to setup and manage Donn Products U.K. A plant was built in the northeast of England near the former coal and steel center of Newcastle. (For musical theater fans, this is where young Billy Elliot danced.) Again, the U.K. government provided a long-term lease/buy on a new factory and grants for equipment and training for the workers. By year three, the U.K. business made money.

Within eight years of starting Donn Germany, Branco hired Walter, the Donn Marketing Superstar discussed elsewhere, to run Donn Scandinavia, located outside of Stockholm. This operation was profitable from its first year.

Twenty years after Branco came on board, Donn Europe had sales of about $40 million (today $80 million) and after tax earnings of $1.5 million (today $3 million) and accounted for over half of Donn's International sales and two thirds of its International profits. All from zero! And due to great choices in people.

The approach was always the same. Start with the people. All the initial ones Branco hired were in their late 30's or 40's and had worked in the building materials industry. They were all self-starters and driven to succeed. All were extremely well paid and had perks like luxury cars plus unlimited travel.

And the European businesses were built with other people's money, to every extent possible. Local, regional, or country development grants, low cost loans and later local bank financing. Very little U.S. funding and even less bank guarantees were provided. Donn in the U.S. provided, and was paid for, its technical know-how with licensing agreements.

This formula can be repeated today for many firms and their products. And if Europe seems dated or you are too late, try somewhere else. But do something Internationally!

Joint Ventures-Trading Technology for Equity

In parts of the world, the Donn approach was to trade their manufacturing and engineering knowhow for an equity position with a large, local partner. Often the partners were in the gypsum business and, like USG Corporation, also manufactured ceiling tiles but they needed a ceiling grid company like Donn. Usually Donn's equity was a minority position like 20% to 33%, which meant you really had no control at the beginning.

When you are a small, startup in Ohio, how do you find these opportunities? As covered in Advisors, you hire someone to help. Donn could not afford the fees of McKinsey but there were alternatives. Don Brown found Bill, a retired British building materials expert, in Bermuda. Bill claimed to know everyone in the world of building materials and he really did.

Donn took a minority position in a business in New Zealand and one in South Africa. Neither investment cost Donn any real cash, it was our ceiling grid knowhow and the people we sent to startup the plants that was our investment. Why this approach and in such remote places?

Donn New Zealand was a partnership with a large N.Z. company, which made the ceiling tiles. New Zealand itself is a very small country but a huge exporter of products to their larger neighbor, Australia, and to the Pacific basin.

Donn New Zealand was very profitable from day one. Over time, Donn in the U.S. received substantial cash dividends as well. Then, based on its profits and assets, we borrowed locally and negotiated the purchase of all the shares from our partner. Today, it remains a profitable business 100% owned by USG.

Donn South Africa was also a partnership with a gypsum company. The country of South Africa has always had very high tariff duties on imported building products so we had had no previous success trying to sell our products there. However, once we setup the venture, it could also export.

We shipped to other parts of the African continent often with favorable import status and no duties. As a result, Donn South Africa made a lot of money. We received cash dividends as well as royalty cash payments for our know-how. Due in part to the legal and political complexities, Donn never did increase its ownership position. But that nominal original investment is worth over $2 million for USG Interiors and the business still operates profitably today.

There are a couple of other learning experiences that came out of our joint venture in South Africa. The country is small, so everyone wants to export their goods elsewhere, particularly

Europe. By setting up this joint venture and technology sharing agreement, Donn was able to legally, limit South Africa from shipping ceiling products into other global areas which Donn serviced. This protects your other businesses and remember we only owned a portion of South Africa' profits not 100%.

The other experience with this joint venture relates to something similar which happened to USG when it participated in a joint venture in Thailand. Same kind of deal, USG gypsum technology and know-how exchanged and a little cash for a minority position. The local partner controlled a gypsum mine. The Thai partner came to USG and requested more money because they wanted to expand the business. Most partnership agreements have a provision that if you cannot put in the new funds required, your equity position gets reduced; in legal jargon, you are diluted. In Advisor jargon, you are screwed!

USG's Thai partner asked for money right around the first USG Financial Crisis, we had none, so the partner now owns the whole company and the USG technology. Not a good deal.

Similarly, Donn S. Africa's partner came to us wanting money to expand the business. We offered our new Access Floor (used in computer rooms) product line and its technology. They loved the idea. They now make that product plus the ceilings. And Donn, now USG, still owns the same equity position. Remember that venture partners, like Advisors, need managing too.

Avoid Global Places beginning with the Letter B

(Expansion that did not work out as planned)

The three worst International expansion projects I can recall were all in places beginning with the letter B. With Donn, Brazil and Beirut, and with USG Interiors, Belgium.

So let's look at some International failures and the reasons for them which can be as helpful as studying successes.

Beirut. Seemed like a good idea. Beirut was called the Paris of the Middle East. So, why not? The Middle East was rapidly growing and needed our ceilings. So we hired a well-respected local manager, as usual, set up a branch, as usual, and a warehouse filled with ceilings, as usual. The war of the early 1980's came and the Donn Beirut warehouse and its products were destroyed; the Manager fled. Goodbye Donn Beirut.

Moral: Do not expand in a political war zone.

Brazil. Hired the Manager. Set up the branch/warehouse. A local competitor convinced the Brazilian government to impose a huge import duty tax just on us. Goodbye Donn Brazil.

Moral: Do better advance homework especially in an emerging market with a different legal system.

Belgium. After USG Corporation acquired Donn, our very successful Donn Europe managers asked us to build a USG Interiors ceiling tile plant in Europe so they could sell the total ceiling package to customers, as we were now able to do in the U.S. This made all the sense in the world and would be a huge success. But somehow the corporate research people at USG had just invented a new, better process to make ceiling tile. Our Donn

Europe managers really only wanted the standard U.S. product, but our new USG corporate bosses and the research group won and the new process and product were built. The government of Belgium threw in a huge development grant. I even presented this large investment to USG's Board of Directors. But the new ceiling tile process never did work as promised. Everyone from USG and the research group tried very hard but the end product was not what the market wanted and the cost advantage never materialized. Goodbye Belgium.

Moral: Do not try a new, unproved technology three thousand miles away from you invented it. And equally important, always try to listen to your local experts.

Chile it's a Country not a Food

When USG acquired Donn, their Chairman, Bob Day, made a major point in the press of how "International" Donn was and how this would help drive USG to become more global. The name USG was an abbreviation for the firm's original name, United States Gypsum Company. And almost everything about the place was United States focused. Oh, there was a good-sized gypsum quarry and drywall plant in Canada, and a smaller version in Mexico. But this was all the "International" USG could claim and accounted for less than 10% of total sales. Donn's International sales were 25% of its total; a very different story from USG.

For decades USG and a handful of other U.S. firms had dominated the domestic gypsum market. The cost of new gypsum material sources and the high cost of building an operating plant created a very high barrier to entry. But by the 1990's, synthetic gypsum from utility plant output provided an alternative raw material. Simultaneously, the recession ended, and a number of smaller manufacturers were forced into bankruptcy or a distressed sale mode. For the first time ever, the U.S. gypsum industry faced an International invasion. Whether they were mining companies from Australia or cement companies from France, they all came looking for a way into the huge, recovering U.S. market. Some of us argued that making USG more international was the way to deal with this threat.

During USG's Financial Crisis, we also tried to find an international investor or partner to help bail us out. Because of the depth of our crisis that did not work. But post-crisis, as the international gypsum players were invading our U.S. market, one of these giant firms came back to us with a proposal for a new international gypsum, joint venture project. And to quote the Godfather, this proposal was an offer too good to refuse.

This international firm was very well known to us from our Financial Crisis investor search. A number of us had met and negotiated with them on several occasions and there was a lot of mutual respect. They were an Asian based forestry and building materials firm. This new project would involve creating a fully integrated gypsum wallboard business in South America, in Chile.

The proposal was for USG to invest a modest amount of cash ($10 million), contribute an old, mothballed plant we had already written off and provide the expertise to get it up and running. They would contribute a local gypsum mine and a distribution firm they had just acquired along with the rest of the required investment and startup funds. We would each own 50% of the mine, plant and distribution company.

This seemed like a very favorable, almost one-sided financial deal in favor of USG. But more importantly, it was the ideal way for the conservative, U.S.-centric USG to make a low cost, low risk entry into the world of real international business.

So we went about assembling a multi-disciplinary team to study this and make a recommendation to the rest of USG's senior management, then to the Board of Directors.

As International business and strategic planning both reported to me, I knew we had to thoroughly investigate and check, in advance, all possible bases and areas of concern to make this project a reality.

So we took the following steps:

–   Name a qualified, trusted Project Leader -a former Donn Canada French speaking controller. Check!

–   Send USG's geology expert to verify the quantity and quality of the local gypsum deposit. Check!

–   Hire a consulting firm to report on the stability and growth prospects of Chile. Check!

–   Have the domestic gypsum group agree on the plant feasibility and buy-in to the project. Check!

–   Review and confirm our partner's financial assumptions and capital returns. Check!

–   Get the whole Team and USG excited. Check!

–   Prepare a full presentation for the Chairman to preview before the Board of Directors. Check!

This whole process took several months and had some interesting moments. We planned to send about a dozen USG people to Chile to perform due diligence. At our kickoff meeting, we discovered that many of the dozen did not have a current passport. Why would they when USG was only in North America? So we quickly got them passports. Everyone was thrilled. We also created a type of project humor. We clarified that Chile was not something you ate at a diner near our Texas gypsum plant. Chile was also not what you felt by Lake Michigan in downtown Chicago on a blustery, winter day. Our Chile was a country! And, by the end of the study, the whole Team was really excited and helped sell the project to the rest of the people at USG headquarters.

I review all this and a draft Board presentation with USG's Chairman. No Check, Chairman not sure.

Have our potential Partner's Group Vice Chairman fly to Chicago to talk to my Chairman. No Check, No Deal.

The potential Partner did the project without USG.

Would one gypsum project in Chile have changed USG forever? Probably not but it could have led to more joint ventures or even solo projects. If successful, it could have helped to change the mindset and the U.S.-centric culture a bit.

Why didn't the USG Chairman want to do this project? I don't recall a specific reason. Maybe he wasn't comfortable with the risk or the venture. The Interiors' Belgium ceiling tile plant was not a success. Maybe he felt the Board would not have given their approval.

But to me and a number of the other senior people involved it was a major disappointment. We did not propose any other International gypsum projects during my short remaining time with the Company.

Eventually, the International guys did invade the U.S. market. Australian, French and even British building material firms bought domestic gypsum plants. USG's market share in the U.S. gradually eroded with all the new competitors.

So sometimes companies and their leaders not have an international state of mind or they are content to just be a major U.S. player.

Newsflash: USG press release February 2014. USG and Australia's Boral Industries announce a new joint venture. USG will contribute its Asian and Middle East businesses, technology and cash and own 50%. Boral will contribute their gypsum group in Australia and Asia. Well, that is more International! This new venture has resulted in a number of senior USG managers now living and travelling extensively in the Far East. Now that is one way to form an International State of Mind!

Lessons Learned from International Business

Develop an International State of Mind:

– If you're born in the large and successful U.S., this is not an easy or natural thing to do

– Can be done with travel and exposure to worldly people; easier when you are young

– As the world changes and U.S. dominance erodes, this can be critical to business survival

Keys to International Business Growth:

– People- hire local, experienced and motivated leaders

– Financial incentives- ownership, top compensation/perks

– Tight timeframe- 2-3 years to achieve profits and positive cash flow or goodbye

– Use other people's money- government grants, regional development programs, local banks

– Leverage one international success off another

– Have a standard approach that fits your business- for Donn it was hire a local manager, setup a branch operation, a warehouse, manufacture locally and then do it again

Consider Minority Owned Joint Ventures:

– Best in remote or culturally difficult areas

– Find a strong, politically connected partner

– Trade your technology/know-how for equity role

– Realize the majority partner is always in control

– Look for chances to enlarge your equity toward 100%

– Avoid equity dilution by offering new, desired technology or product line or territory

– Protect your majority owned International locations

Avoid Common International Mistakes:

– Minimize U.S. expatriates

– Make sure your senior locals speak your language almost as well as their own

– Avoid social/political areas prone to revolt/war

– Remember that corrupt or influx legal systems can disadvantage new entries

– Stay clear of countries that begin with "B" or whatever pattern does not work for you

– Don't introduce a new, unproven product or process thousands of miles from your base

When trying to introduce International expansion in a large, U.S.-centric company:

– Pick an initial project/venture/location with a high potential for success
– Assemble a well-respected team
– Make it a fun challenge especially for first time International members
– Get your Team to sell the project for you
– Cover all Bases. Political, Social, Technical, Financial and Operational
– Never assume your CEO/Senior Team is on board
– Create opportunities for your senior people to travel and live outside of the U.S. like in USG's new joint venture

Remember it is difficult to overcome a bias against International but it can be done with the right Leaders.

But also remember the old adage, which we modify here: Grow International or Perish!

And most important, if You want to be Global and your Company does not- Leave!

9. Charts and Systems
(Or What is Really Important)

Introduction to Charts and Systems

This will not be a technical discussion about the current level of Information Systems in companies, although I have had, several CIOs (Chief Information Officers), along with their groups of people, and expensive hardware/software, report to me. Nor will this be a review of Sarbanes Oxley's requirements for an elaborate system of internal controls so that our Congress can try, in vain, to avoid another Enron. After our discussion on Management Fraud, you learned that it is people not systems and procedures that cause and solve most fraud problems.

That said, we will touch on a smattering of topics that explore how companies try to manage and control their businesses. As with many of our stories, we will learn about some things that work and help people and their business succeed, and even become part of a firm's culture. And, of course, some practices that tend to impede the firm and its employees. Along the way we may even touch on what is really important.

Let's start by looking at Charts. Organization ones.

Charts that Guide your Future vs. Recording your Past

Accountants like charts like Consultants like Charts. Accountants use them to point out good and bad things to management. Consultants use them to sell their view, thus their fees, to others. Charts can take on many different roles but sometimes they can change your whole life.

Smart or Lucky, How a Chart got me Hired at Donn

My old boss George used to ask this question: Would you rather be smart or lucky, if you could only pick one?

One day as we are working on this book, I tell this story to my writing coach/friend Cheryl. She immediately asks, what is the best example of this I can think of in my own career? Answer, how I was hired by Donn.

As a new Arthur Andersen Audit Senior assigned for the first time to Donn, I was trying to get my head around all the legal and structural changes Donn was undergoing.

In the past year, Europe had gone from the German firm to a new operation in France, with the United Kingdom next. Donn U.S. had purchased two access floor companies. But the most changes had occurred in the modular housing group.

Since all these businesses-regardless of their exact legal structure or ownership percentage-were under the Donn umbrella, they all had to be audited. And most of this new, upcoming audit work had to be done by me in our Cleveland office. Your first year is hard enough on a new audit client but Donn was like a moving target. As was my practice when faced with a complex situation, I asked questions and looked at legal documents.

I created a chart and labeled it, "Donn Chart of Companies and Relationships." Starting with Donn Corporation at the top, it went down through the Canadian, U.S. and European businesses showing the existing companies and below them, their new businesses. The modular housing section had arrows going all over the place because that was how it was organized with overlapping and horizontal corporations and partnerships.

The Donn Chart was not a finished work of art rather it was a starting point to help me organize the audit. First, I had to ensure it accurately reflected the facts. I took the Donn Chart to Kathy, George's assistant, explained what it was and asked if she could have George look at it and make any corrections. She came over to my room later and said that George thought the Chart was great and, with my permission, she will type it up for George, Donn's outside lawyers and some others. Would I like a copy? Sure... My Chart becomes "The Official Donn Corporation Chart."

That was the first real encounter I ever had with George and it caught his attention in a positive way. At the end of the very long Donn Audit that year, George offered me a job at Donn. I accepted and had some of the most enjoyable career and personal times of my life. So was it smart to draw up a Chart to make my own job workable or lucky to show it to George that day? If you only get one choice, pick lucky every time.

Congratulations you appear on Chart 1A!

After USG Corporation acquired Donn Corporation, we formed what USG called Integration Committees. The stated purposes of the Committees were two-fold: to help integrate Donn into USG, especially all its corporate groups, and to assist with the merger of Donn and the other USG businesses into the newly formed USG Interiors. Something like 24 Committees were created.

From the USG side, totally different people were on each Integration Committee. For example, there were three Committees related to legal matters all headed by separate VPs - Corporate, Secretary and Labor. From Donn, which had no inside legal professionals, I was the representative(s). There was a similar series of financial Committees. USG's Treasurer headed matters like cash management and taxes. The USG Controller headed internal audit, monthly and SEC reporting. Donn, had limited financial professionals-myself, my corporate guy, Dale, or our U.S. Controller, Al, were on multiple Committees. The same was true of Human Resources, Benefits and the Pension Committees and on and on. There were plenty of USG corporate officers to be on these never ending Committees and just a few of us Donn people.

The USG officers and their other Committee members seemed to have plenty of time to meet. But we Donn people had full-time jobs trying to run our worldwide company, which USG had just acquired, plus the important task of trying to pull together this new group called USG Interiors.

In an integration process like this, you learn a lot about the systems for each firm and what is important in their culture. At the initial meeting of each new Committee, the USG people would hand the Donn people a giant stack of forms or written policies. For example, the Code of Business Conduct that each USG employee signed each year. Each time the USG people would ask us for our forms or policies. Invariably, Donn had none or very little. Often, each side would stare at the other in total disbelief. Disbelief for the Donn people that USG would waste the time and effort in designing forms or procedures for every single thing. Disbelief for the USG people that Donn had such a disregard for the importance of forms and procedures for almost every single thing. Very different company cultures.

At an early HR meeting, I was handed the "USG Corporation and its Subsidiaries Management Organization Charts." It was a book, literally of about 110 pages of charts. The charts were organized by who reported to whom. Units reporting to the CEO vs. those reporting to the then Vice Chairman etc. The USG CFO alone had 8 charts. I knew I had a problem when asked for the Donn book of Charts. I went back to Ohio and, with my assistant Kathy helping, we created a dozen charts for the Donn worldwide companies. Our Donn U.S. business, which the oldest and largest part, actually had a current set of another dozen charts. So Donn and I looked better by the second meeting.

The true meaning of the USG Organization Charts was drilled into me a year later when USG Interiors was officially created from Donn and other USG companies. At USG, the head financial person in a business reported to a corporate group CEO not to his business President. The group CEOs reported to the USG Chairman on Chart #1. As the head financial guy for the new Interiors group, I ended up on Chart #1A. I might not have noticed, but one of my new Interiors friends, a lifetime USG guy named Alton comes up to me and with his Oklahoma drawl, says:

- Brad, for a guy who has only been around a few months, you have already accomplished one of my 30 years goals!
- I respond, what is that goal, Alton?
- Well, Brad, You are on Chart #1A !

At USG, charts, systems and procedures were king!

Can you guess who produced and kept tight control on the distribution of the USG Management Organization book of charts?

My father would say, I will give you three guesses and the first two won't count. It was our corporate Human Resource friends. Most all the USG charts, forms and procedures were created and managed by the various corporate groups like legal, HR and finance. These forms can have value but only if they help run the real businesses, not to as a way to provide control or oversight by a lot of corporate staff.

$10 Bills and the Weekly Tapes (Not about Numbers!)

When I first arrived at Donn, I found what we would now call an ancient cassette tape recorder on my desk. My assistant, Kathy, told me that it could be used for occasional dictation. But it was also to be used for Donn's owner, Don Brown, and his weekly taped reports. Every Friday, Mr. Brown's assistant, Jane, gave you a specially made blank tape with three minutes of recordable time.

After you made your recording you returned the tape to Jane and were given a $10 bill (another Donn Incentive). She would then record the individual tapes onto a large reel that Mr. Brown would listen to over the weekend. There were some 50 people scattered throughout the company, sometimes four layers down, who recorded these tapes that only Don Brown heard. Each person turned in 50 tapes a year and received $500, which somehow, in those early years, was not exactly recorded in the payroll system. (Another great reward!)

So I understood the mechanics of the weekly tape system but what to record for Don Brown? I asked one of the few other financial people in the company. He says, your title is Corporate Controller, you can let Mr. Brown know how the sales or profits are going and stuff like that.

So for my first few months, I report numbers.

Then the Controller of the Modular Housing business quits and I was asked to go to their plant and help out. Upon my arrival, it was obvious that we have major problems with this business. Their current housing project was way behind schedule and they had little, useful information to help manage the situation as this was, again, a one-time project.

The people working in the plant and the small office also seemed to sense things were going from bad to worse. Then on Friday, I had another problem. My blank weekly tape somehow followed me to the Modular plant. There was really no traditional financial information or numbers I could report to Mr. Brown. After a brief internal debate, I recorded my first week observations of what was going on at the plant. The high level of confusion, the low level of morale and the tense relationships between several key managers. It seemed easy and natural to do, as talking privately into the recorder was like a one-way stream of consciousness. And it took less research and outlining than my normal, more structured, numbers based reports. I continued this approach for the next several weeks at the plant. This was easier and there was no other real option.

Then one Friday, a note from Jane, "Mr. Brown said your recent reports were excellent, keep up the good work!"

My temporary assignment at the Modular plant was on and off for the next five years even after we hired a new Controller. I found myself having lunch alone with Mr. Brown on a regular basis and working on all his other high priority projects. From the day of that Friday note, I rarely included numbers in my weekly tapes. Maybe once a year when the annual audit was complete. Or about the bank loan during Donn's Financial Crisis. But Don Brown did not care about that; he cared about people and their relationships to each other and the business. In the end, it's not about the numbers.

If the Donn Chart of Companies helped get me noticed and hired by George at Donn, it was the weekly tapes that gave me the opportunity to work directly with Don Brown.

Smart or Lucky? Both!

An Early Adaptor of Voicemail

The weekly message systems to Don Brown were always evolving. Since the weekly cassette tapes were slow and limiting, Mr. Brown began working with several electronics and phone companies. We filled a storage area with recorders which all had separate dial-in numbers. Most of these attempts cost Donn Corporation money along the way even if we were partnering with a major vendor.

Somehow Don Brown talked his way into becoming a beta test site for Octel, one of the very early leaders in the emerging voicemail business. As a result, by the early 1980's, the mid-sized Donn Corp. had a full, operational voicemail system for all its managers and sales force. With this, Mr. Brown could not only receive his weekly reports, he could play them individually at his leisure, replay, or save certain ones. So Don Brown could manage the way he liked, verbally, not in writing. All this occurred years or even a decade before many larger, or even more technology driven businesses, installed such systems. And all of us were required to learn several generations of voicemail just to get our $10 bills! So we became very comfortable with this great tool well before our personal or business peers. When USG Corporation acquired Donn; one of the few Donn systems it immediately adopted was the Donn voicemail system. And USG was ten times our size.

IBM Personal Computers, Another Donn Incentive!

In late 1981, IBM introduced what would become the world's first popular personal computer or PC. At the time, Donn like most companies was processing all its data on mid-sized computers like Hewlett Packard or main frames by IBM. But sensing that this new PC could become a powerful business tool, Don Brown's son, Keith, sponsored a novel plan to help the Company leapfrog into the future. Another Donn Incentive!

The first PC setup cost about $4000 then (over $9000 in today's dollars). There were no laptops; only desktops and you needed a separate processor, monitor, phone modem and cables. The Donn Incentive plan was offered to the top 100 managers and worked like this.

You would agree to forfeit $4000 of your annual bonus in exchange for your own personal computer. We withheld taxes of about $2000 (rates were higher then). So, at this point the PC setup cost you $2000 of your cash. But in the true spirit of the Browns, you could earn that $2000 back by creating at home, two simple business applications we could use at the Company. So we all opt in and create things like sales call reports, monthly property insurance reports or whatever.

In doing this before today's icon driven, touch screen programs you actually learned something about programming in now forgotten computer languages like DOS or Basic and how to operate a personal computer. You also learned about memory cards, graphic boards and modem speeds. At that point, the only

Mouse anyone knew of lived at Disney World so you even had to learn computer commands to make everything work.

The first PCs and their software was slow and primitive, but again, all the Donn managers were on the leading edge of the new personal computing revolution. Our early exposure to this world made us better adaptors and less fearful of what came next.

If Donn were still around, the Browns would have made a deal with Apple for the first iPads or the latest iPhone model as part of some new incentive plan. And if the Browns had met Steve Jobs, Donn could have been a test site for whatever other new thing he was creating. You can bet on it!

The Value of Using New Technology

The real beneficiaries of these incentives and this willingness to try new technologies were the Donn and, later, the USG businesses. For USG, it started with Donn's voicemail.

When we formed USG Interiors, we took eight PCs to Chicago, more than in all of USG. We brought a financial reporting and consolidation system for Interiors, which ran on PCs and ended up being used by the whole organization. Donn sales, manufacturing and engineering people brought similar systems.

USG really benefited from acquiring a group of people who were willing and comfortable using changing, new technologies.

Bottom line, sometimes big companies just need a push to move into advanced technology because initially, that technology does not fit in with their normal comfort zone of Charts and Systems.

Lessons Learned from Charts and Systems

Charts and Systems in a business tend to:
- Reflect a company's culture and tend to be either open and flexible or rigid and controlling
- Also reflect what is really important to the Owner or Founder or CEO of a business

If given the choice of smart or lucky, pick Lucky!

Learn the importance of your company's systems but do not let them keep you from doing what is best for the business.

Find creative ways and incentives to encourage staff to learn today's new technologies and you will benefit greatly.

Learn that numbers are always less important than people whether in a weekly report or a meeting.

Some Charts and Systems:
- Help people and their businesses work better
- Impede individuals and team success
- Allow big companies to learn from smaller organizations

10. Board of Directors

(We all Report to Someone)

Introduction

Fortune Magazine published an article a couple years ago on British Petroleum and the disaster in the Gulf. Headline, "Who's to Blame, start with its top-notch Board." The article points out that after a series of terrible accidents in Texas and Alaska, the Board knew for years that safety was a major issue. Internal reports stated that the Company's prevailing culture was saving money first, and safety second. The article notes that the BP Board was comprised of current and former CEOs. So why did these safety disasters keep occurring? Here's why: people in companies focus on what they believe are really important to their leaders and the Board is the final Boss. Employees figure this out and act accordingly. For BP it was lower cost vs. safety.

At USG Corporation, safety was not only a core value, it was the primary core value. USG started out as a firm mining gypsum for use in their wallboard products. Safety performance is talked about constantly, not just in posters. At business group staff meetings, safety statistics are the first order of business. And this goes on in the Board meetings as well. Whenever there was a serious accident, yet alone a death, we, as Senior Management and the Board would look at diagrams and sometimes grisly photos of exactly what happened and why.

The local plant or operating site staff would often lose their entire annual incentive bonus because of a serious accident. Safety was a very positive cultural trait that USG brought to Donn. When a plant reached a safety milestone, like one million hours worked accident-free, it was publicized and celebrated, often at a dinner with spouses.

I and other senior officers attended these dinners at USG and IMC Global, because it really was important. Safety, like many business issues must be drilled into people in a consistent manner until everyone understands, and believes it is important. Certainly this was the case at USG; at BP, hopefully, it will be.

Now we could spend days or weeks looking at headlines about Boards of Directors and their troubles. But instead let's focus on some situations where Boards can do things right and look at some broad guidelines for how public and private Boards should operate.

Why is this worthwhile? People in business or other organizations look both at and up to their leaders. At the top of any leadership world is the Board of Directors so Boards need to function better. Let's start with a lesser-known concept of Boards in private companies.

Private Company Boards

You might ask why a private company would even have a Board unless it was owned by a number of individuals or other companies. But private company Boards can assist even single owners or families in a variety of ways, as we will see.

Private joint ventures (JVs): As we discussed under International, JVs often have Boards of Directors to give the different owners (whether individuals or corporations) a voice on major matters such as capital expenditures, acquisitions or appointing a President. Usually the number of Directors is small, five or less, and seats are allocated to the controlling owners based on their ownership percentage. Donn Corporation's many joint ventures all had that structure whether it was New Zealand, South Africa or Saudi Arabia. For example, in Donn South Africa, Donn owned one third of the JV and had one of the three Directors. The Directors named on these private, JV Boards were almost always senior officers from each corporation that owned the venture. Thus there was never a question on whether a Director had industry knowledge, was competent, or involved.

Over the years, I represented Donn and later, USG, on a number of these private venture Boards that would meet annually or as needed. Usually these Boards had a good set of partnership or joint venture rules that worked well, providing the operating company with autonomy and the controlling corporations with oversight on major matters. That is what good Boards should do to achieve corporate governance.

Even wholly owned private firms find that Boards of Directors can add real value for a variety of reasons. Let's look at a couple of very different examples.

Donn Corporation Management Boards: Donn's founder, Don Brown, needed to get his sons more involved with the business and with the senior managers who were running things. He did this by establishing Management Boards. We set up Boards for the holding company and each of the various worldwide businesses-U.S., Canada, Europe and the rest of International. The senior officer in each area, like the famous Branco from Europe, was named the Chairman and could add his senior people to the Board. Don Brown and his sons, along with myself and others were added from the corporate group. The new element was that the heads of additional areas like the U.S. or Canada were also added to the Donn Europe Management Board. This was quite revolutionary for the very private Donn Corporation. Why?

Previously, operating or financial results were never shared between Donn's various worldwide businesses. But this new approach enabled fresh marketing ideas from Europe to be picked up quickly by the other locations. And when the technology leading U.S. business was considering a new ceiling grid design, which would require expensive new tooling to manufacture, the smaller Canadian or European groups could decide when they would follow suit and how they would introduce the new product.

As I said, Don Brown's other motivation was to use this Board process as a way to insert his adult sons more deeply into the various businesses which by now were all large, successful, and managed by very independent, strong willed people. Donn's senior managers would be respectful, and generally cooperative, to Don Brown and financial guys like George and me because we helped them make money, or avoid jail time for tax issues, but they had little time for anyone else. Remember Donn's worldwide Presidents were kings.

The Donn Management Boards did a very good job of getting the worldwide senior management more involved and up to speed on the total Donn business. They also helped provide more exposure for Don Brown's sons. But before any other major impact could occur, Donn Corporation was sold to USG and the Management Boards were gone.

Duraflow Industries Advisors: But you do not need to be a large, international private company to benefit from Board-like Advisors. We have a young, entrepreneur friend, Mark, who has a startup manufacturing business. Mark's father, who I have known for years, sensed his son needed some help. I met Mark and was impressed with how he handled himself and his business. He did need help and some specialized input outside of my base. I reached out to an old sales friend, Bob, and a technical guy, Ron, both from Donn Corporation and both recently retired. Within a short time, Duraflow had an idle, but valuable, piece of equipment working with a mocked up trouble-shooting guide from Ron. Bob, in a coaching role, went on a couple sales calls with Mark. Bob also brought in a local college professor whose MBA class created a first time Duraflow Strategic Plan. Mark wisely keeps us in the loop with emails and asks our opinion on matters that range from a new credit application form to a second MBA class project. We also advised Mark to join a peer networking, business group like YPO, Young Presidents Organization. What does all this cost

Mark and his small company? Nothing. What does Duraflow gain from over 100 combined years of business experience? Mark would tell you, Priceless! Should most small companies build an Advisor network? Yes. What about Boards at public firms.

Public Company Boards

The Perceived vs. Real Power of Directors: It was explained to me by my lawyer friend, Frank, on one of our walks to St. Patrick's Cathedral to pray for USG Corporation that in the world of public companies, "Management serves at the pleasure of the Board." I was never sure why he told me this; we already had enough pressure trying to save USG. But the phrase has stuck with me for several reasons. First, it is, of course, true; in a public firm, Shareholders elect the Board and the Board names and elects the Chairman/CEO, and all those other C level people (Yes, even HR) plus all titled Officers.

Likewise, the Board can choose not to elect someone as an Officer or just replace him or her. This sounds very powerful. Which brings us to our second point. In reality, the Chairman/CEO recommends whom they want elected and in 99+% of cases, the Board elects these people with very little discussion. That is the way it works for most officers. This is a shame as one of the Board's key duties involves management succession.

The time this "serves at the pleasure" phrase really has meaning is when the Board needs to remove/replace the seated Chairman/CEO as Hewlett Packard has repeatedly done. Ironically, when that occurs, it is not a pleasure for HP or any Board. It is painful and a lot of work.

But regardless of the perceived or real power of the Board, many corporate Officers are afraid of their Directors. This is stupid. Directors should be treated like any other superior you report to; answer their questions in a respectful tone, correct their many and frequent misconceptions without embarrassing them and look directly at them while speaking.

Fear, by any company's Officer, can be sensed and this is not good around wild animals like mockingbirds, rats, or human Directors. Even my lawyer friend, Frank, agrees with that.

Qualifications for Directors, the One Third Rule

One Third of Directors are not qualified to serve for a variety of reasons: no relevant background, too old, no interest, too clueless. I have been on Board phone conference calls when a Director falls asleep and snores. Or when a Director goes off on a long, unannounced break and you ask a question that sounds like the tree falling in the empty forest. Or they do not know how to mute their phone and go to a nearby kitchen to make a snack or worse, a nearby, open-doored bathroom. (How I wish these things were just made up!)

Another issue is Directors from academia, nonprofits or government. Again many of these are great people. One of my public companies had a wonderful Director from one of these areas. The Director was the head of one of our key Committees. One day he told me that he had once managed a department with a budget of $20 million. My information systems budget alone was larger, yet alone the treasury and controller groups or the billions of company debt I managed. Different worlds.

Boards are now adopting rules on age limits and are trying to be more selective with their choices. Perhaps we can lower this Director group to 25% but for now it's still one third.

Another One Third of all Directors are actually qualified to serve but are too busy with their own job, on too many Boards or just not interested and thus contribute almost nothing. These Directors are harder to spot because of their resumes. Many attend most meetings and appear alive and awake but you can tell they are usually not prepared. The Board materials we spent days (and nights) preparing and sending to them ahead, are left home because they haven't looked at it.

Many do not ask any questions about anything during the meeting. Some regularly ask how long the meeting should take. Other Directors serve for the pleasure of the Board lunches. Still others can spend your entire Board dinner regaling everyone with a story about another company's issues or their latest trip on their corporate business jet. They would qualify as masters in the art of Lunches and Dinners.

A Director at IMC Global for a brief time, who at 90+ is still very busy, was Henry Kissinger. Apple has a Director who ran for President, invented the internet, proved weather changes and like Dr. Kissinger, won the Nobel Peace Prize. As a general suggestion, Directors who win Nobel Prizes may be too busy to serve on your Board. But this group can also include real corporate CEOs who seem like they could be helpful. We had one Director who "accidentally" joined one of our major competitor Boards because their meeting dates worked better for him and then he abruptly had to resign from our Board. Talk about a conflict of interest! So look hard and do real research before naming a Director. It is a very important job.

Which brings us to the last One Third of Directors of public Boards who are qualified, do the work, and contribute by serving the companies that hired them. In the typical public Board of 12 members, this active Director group numbers 3 or 4. At meetings, this One Third does most of the talking, asks almost all of the questions and may occasionally even raise their voices. Often, these are current or former CEOs or CFOs who are not shy and want to receive real answers to their questions. As a member of Management you need to ascertain just who these Directors are and make sure you have them on your side on new incentive plans, major capital projects, acquisitions, etc.

In the USG Financial Crisis we had regular pre-meetings with Directors especially those on the Finance Committee before an important Board vote. Sometimes, this group will even disagree with Management on a Board agenda item and get the rest of the Board on their side. Of course, the best Directors I have ever worked with come from this active One Third. When times are tough, these are the only Directors you really want to have!

So why is this active One Third group of Directors outnumbered and encumbered by the rest? The selection process for Directors is partially to blame. Most public Boards have a Committee on Directors whose job it is to nominate Directors. Who do these Directors usually nominate? People they know.

From where? Other public Boards! In a city, even one as large as Chicago, this results in a lot of overlapping directors on each other's Boards. For example, for a number of years USG's former Chairman/CEO was on the Board of Chicago based transportation company GATX. Now GATX's Chairman is on USG's Board.

Remember, familiarity does not improve Board's effectiveness. Open dialogue does.

There is another even deeper, core problem with Board effectiveness. We could call it cronyism or the old boy network but it goes beyond all this. Often, senior executives, get to the top by being overly polite and not offending other senior bosses along the way. Some of these Leaders can avoid strong opinions or difficult decisions for most of their careers. Again, this is a shame because to fulfill one's duty as a Director, sometimes negative input or disagreements with the Chairman is critical.

So when these types of Chairman go on each other's Boards the same thing occurs. Chairman/CEOs who do not like to be criticized themselves, do not criticize the Chairman/CEO who invites them to be on their Board (since a public firm director annually earns $150,000 plus per a recent Hewitt study).

Many of these Directors, fall in the middle One Third who should be useful but are not. Again with all the recent corporate failures, Boards are being scrutinized as never before and are reevaluating their Director criteria so perhaps going forward this will improve. But then again we started by looking at a giant company, BP, with an impressive, at least on paper, Board. But were all these BP and other Directors worth it to the companies they were hired to serve?

We can't be sure. So how can public Boards be improved?

Public Board Sizes and Mix, Less can be Better

A lot has been written about the size of Boards and the mix of insiders (the firm's executives) vs. outsiders (independent Directors). Much has changed over the last couple decades. Twenty-five years ago, USG had 15 Directors, 5 or 33% were officers. Now USG has 9 Directors only 1 is an officer.

A most successful company, Apple, has only 8 Directors with only 1 insider. BP had 13 Directors with 3 (23%) insiders.

So what is the right mix and number of Directors? The less the better. You want involved Directors who can be on Committees and be active participants. Studies show the best number of Directors is 9-10 and I agree. And how many insiders? At the most, 2 out of 10 or 20%. Just make sure the outsiders are good ones who really want to serve on your Board.

A Final Word on Boards

Leadership, we are rightly told, starts at the top. The Board of Directors is as top as it gets in the world of public companies or many private firms and even nonprofits.

Directors and Boards need to set an example and actually lead the firm. Not agreeing to everything management proposes and learning to say no more often would be a great start.

Senior Management needs to be open with their Board and view them as a resource, not a necessary evil.

Lessons Learned from Board of Directors

The Board needs to believe in priorities, like safety, before the workers will believe in it.

Whether it's your first exposure to a Director or your ongoing role, know your material and present it with confidence, not fear.

Private firms should consider a small Board with interested, trusted, knowledgeable Directors.

Private company Advisors or Directors can provide inexpensive business insight even for startups.

Fear can be sensed and has no place in a Boardroom.

Boards can no longer retain Directors who are unqualified due to background/age/anything even if they own a block of stock or are nice!

Boards must remove or retrain qualified Directors who could serve but do not, regardless of why.

Real research and diligence should go into naming Directors not just another Director's referral.

Public Boards should increase their One Third qualified and involved Directors to Two Thirds and then to 100%.

Board size is best kept small-under 10 with 2 Insiders.

Leadership starts at the top, Directors must lead by example and learn to say No!

Senior Management must learn to view the Board as an Asset not a Liability.

With all the talk of Board reform these days, there is still a long way to go. Let's start now!

11. Planning

(In Business and Life)

Planning is everywhere and sometimes, everything. In our personal world, we plan our days, struggle to plan our careers and try in vain to plan our children's choices and lives. In business, digital devices allow or force us to schedule our time in fifteen-minute intervals. Software now easily accommodates ongoing business forecasts that we used to struggle with.

Some people might wonder if, in our current age of endless data, we even need to plan. After all, our iPhone can give us a list of restaurants and make reservations with no preplanning. At work our laptops can keep us linked to our business on a 24/7 basis.

So do we really need to plan? OF COURSE, WE DO! In this and later sections, we will show what good and bad Planning can help you accomplish and also avoid.

In companies, Strategic Planning and Mergers and Deals all go together and sometimes get out of their natural order. But Planning should always go first.

Let's look at a framework for Planning.

A Planning Model for Business and Life

We'll start with a multi-step definition or model which can be used in business or life. First, we will look at Planning in a big picture or strategic way, then we will look at the alternatives we have to consider, and finally, we will select a course of action and do something. In business, this last step often results in a major transaction (an asset sale, a merger or a financing). In life, it means making a definite, conscious choice for action. When these 3 steps are done, we will go back to the beginning and look at the situation in its new form. Remember, the 3 steps keep going continuously.

Philosophy/Approach toward Planning as a Continuum

Webster defines continuum as "a coherent whole, characterized as a sequence or progression of elements." That is how proper Planning should occur. Planning in business is a continuous process with three distinct but linked activities: traditional strategic planning, a review of strategic alternatives, and implementation of specific policies, programs, or transactions. Planning is also not a one time or static activity. Rather, it is an iterative process focused on an ever moving, continuous, circular target. Thus the continuum; Planning is a whole process with a sequence but when you think you are at the end, you need to circle back to the beginning and update your results. Let's start by looking at its three distinct but linked parts.

First step *Traditional strategic planning*. This has been taught in MBA programs for years. A number of great frameworks exist from scholars like Harvard's Michael Porter, to McGill's Henry Mintzberg, and Jim Collins from Stanford. We can also learn from our Advisor friends like McKinsey and their classic 7S format. Traditional strategic planning should always make you define organizational goals, analyze your industry and its trends, and competitors' strengths and weaknesses versus your own. From this beginning, you can define some broad strategic issues as well as more specific operating issues for your business. Let's do a short version, for a building products company like Donn, to show this more vividly:

Main Goals:

- Become #1 worldwide in all product lines
- Double sales in 3 years; profits in 5 years

Industry:

- Commercial construction trend up/down
- National/local building codes/standards
- Expanded emphasis on recycled materials

Competitors:

- Other private firms, Chicago Metallic
- Public firms, Armstrong, international

Company:

- Strengths: private, informal style, geographic/product range
- Weaknesses: limited funding, lack of internal controls
- Strategic and Operating Issues: broad items like retaining family ownership to specific items for sales, manufacturing
- Financials: Detail annual plan and 5 year forecast

You get the idea. Each of Donn's worldwide businesses would prepare a Strategic Plan like this every year and we would review them in the Management Board meetings. This Meeting would be dedicated solely to the Strategic Plan and could take a full day depending on the issues and the amount of questions. Each group's President and key reports would be involved and their Controller would wrap up with the financial projections. That is the first part of Planning, the traditional Strategic Plan.

The second step is to *Review Strategic Alternatives*. A well thought out Strategic Plan should lead the Company and its key managers to this next step, looking at the different choices or actions to prioritize and evaluate. In the USG Financial Crisis we went over a thorough example of this. The Key Strategic Issue was financial survival and we investigated a number of alternatives:

– Search for an industry or financial investor using our Bankers' networks and almost did a deal with Sam Zell

– Sell major Assets like the USG HQ Building and a non-core business, DAP; these were done.

– Explore an out-of-court debt restructuring with the banks and bondholders; this was not possible since it would require 100% agreement of all debtors

– We did execute a holding company only bankruptcy while converting over $1 billion of debt into equity

This wide range of options, which we actually reviewed, is typical. What was not typical is that it took three years. But this is what Alternative Strategic Reviews are all about. You look at as wide a range of choices as possible. And, you often eliminate an alternative for one reason or another. But we were prepared to do something different because we had evaluated all options.

The third step in the Planning process is *Asset/Capital Transactions*. This involves actually completing a significant transaction. In terms of Assets, it can be an acquisition of another company or its operating assets like USG buying Donn. Asset transactions can also include the sale or divestiture of a business or of major non-operating assets like USG selling its headquarters building, or its DAP business to raise critical cash. Capital Transactions can range from Donn's private placement of bonds with insurance companies to USG's total re-do of its debt and stock. All of these transactions should be tied to the Strategic Plan and should occur after you have evaluated all your alternatives. Often one transaction like selling an asset triggers a capital transaction like paying down debt.

For now, the point remains that Planning is a continuum; you barely get the plan written and you better be Planning what will happen next because business, like life, keeps changing. Planning is an iterative process, focused on a moving target and it looks like this:

Strategic Plan > Broad Objectives > Specific Actions and Results > Leads you to Modify the Strategic Plan

So Why Bother Planning if it Keeps Changing?

We have all seen one of those management or self-help posters that say, "If you don't know where you are going, any path will take you there." And that is true.

The reason individuals, businesses, not-for-profits and yes, even governments, should Plan is to create a baseline or base case, of sorts, with which to compare their actual progress. The Plan also provides you with a reference when things get out of line or out of control. This is why healthy people have their blood pressure checked regularly, and get annual physical exams. Organizations need this type of baseline as well. For example, most states require condominium associations to have an annual meeting, review a budget for the next year, project future common repairs like roofs and painting, and provide cash reserves to deal with these items.

When Donn was small, Planning consisted of a one year earnings forecast. As Donn grew, this became multi-year forecasts of earnings, cash flow and the balance sheet. Later, Donn was doing quarterly rolling forecasts; larger firms like USG often do monthly forecasts. But Planning is not just about the numbers. Planning is after all, an ever-changing continuum.

So Who Needs to be Involved in the Planning?

Everyone. That is right, Everyone.

To do Planning right, everyone in the firm should participate in creating or reviewing parts of the Plan. Obviously it depends on how you are organized and whether you are very private, like Donn or very public, like USG. But the general rule: the more people involved, the better the Plan.

The real value is having the widest possible input, and thus ideas, into the plan and when it's complete, the widest possible distribution for ownership or buy-in of the Plan. Planning should not be limited to the line or operating people but include staff groups. Planning is also best not handled at corporate headquarters but at the lowest level from which valid input can be gained for the Plan.

Lastly, Can Planning impact my Personal Life?

If you were paying attention, you know the answer is Yes.

Daniel Levinson, from Yale, examined adult development in his book, The Seasons of a Man's Life. The book categorizes, by age group, the stages of adult development we all go through. I have given out dozens of copies of the book to men and women friends and everyone raves about how helpful it was.

So why talk about it here? Well, one of the major findings in the book involves Planning. Levinson found everyone, every five years, consciously or subconsciously, analyzes and re-evaluates all parts of his or her lives- personal, career, and education. Then we either decide to keep going with what or who we are, or we decide to change that part of our life. We do this by thinking about Key Issues and Objectives, by Reviewing our Strategic Alternatives and by Executing activities for change.

Doesn't that sound a lot like Strategic Planning, its three distinct, but linked parts, and the fact that Planning is a continuum which is constantly in motion? You got it!

If you have learned to Plan, you can learn to make Deals.

Lessons Learned from Planning

Planning, strategic or otherwise, is everywhere.

Planning and Deals go together but proper Planning can minimize bad Deals and maximize good Deals.

Planning has three distinct but linked parts:
1. Traditional strategic planning using various frameworks
2. Review of strategic alternatives or options
3. Asset/capital transactions
   - Assets: buy/sell, expand/downsize
   - Capital: stock or debt choices

Planning is a continuum that often changes rapidly.

Planning, like a medical exam, gives you a base to compare future results and helps make decisions when a crisis occurs.

Even not-for-profits and small, private firms can benefit from Planning to manage and improve their activities.

Everyone possible should be involved in Planning's input and review of the final result.

Staff groups, not just line or operating groups should be involved in and benefit from Planning.

OK, we have planned enough; let's do some Deals!

12. Mergers and Deals
(Someone Bought; Someone Sold)

Dreaming about Deals

Much of my working career was occupied with Mergers and Deals. Even the Donn and USG Financial Crisis we covered were really about trying to negotiate a Deal. During the rapidly growing Donn years, most of the Deals consisted of us buying or acquiring others. During the downsizing at USG and IMC Global, most of the Deals consisted of selling or divestitures.

Bankers, Lawyers and other Advisors keep track of their Deals for their resume. Bankers also help clients keep score of their Deals with Lucite reminders called tombstones, which they buy in bulk and joyously hand them out to anyone who was ever near a Deal. Having received dozens of these, I only keep two: the USG Financial Crisis and the actual sale of Donn to USG.

And, I have never kept a list of my Deals for several reasons. First, my priority in a Deal was to help my company either grow by buying things or to fight for its survival by selling things. Second, although many Wizard Advisors act as if any successful Deal is due solely to their involvement, some of us view these major transactions more as a team effort. The number of Deals or their size was not how I chose to measure myself. Rather, it was the impact the Deal had on my Company.

Ultimately, you realize that much of business and life revolves around Mergers and Deals. Deals are, after all, about negotiating. And we negotiate constantly in business and life.

Even though I don't count my Deals, I dream about Deals regularly. Often, I am part of a group in some unrecognizable conference room with at least one, revolving person from my past but that person is not necessarily from any particular Deal. Some of these known people are no longer living, like my old bosses George or Gene. We are listening to unknown, young Wizard Advisors, present some bizarre theory and, as in the daylight world, no one is really paying attention.

In the dreams, I always try to help solve the problem or break the logjam sometimes over meals. At times the subject seems familiar and at other times I wake up wondering how I could ever have dreamed up that type of business or its issues. Usually, after working hard on the Deal, I suddenly realize that I no longer work for this company so why am I even there? Then I wake up. Deals can be powerful stuff and aspects or issues can live on even in your dreams.

To paraphrase the Joni Mitchell song, I have looked at Deals from "Both Sides Now," from buying and selling others to being bought and sold myself but I really don't know Deals at all!

So, we will try to look at them from a number of sides.

You Lose a Lot Even in Good Mergers and Deals

In my hometown of Cleveland, a Huntington Bank clerk found a box of cancelled checks from the old Union Commerce Bank. There were checks written and signed by 23 former Presidents including Lincoln the day before he was killed. The box had been forgotten since the bank takeover thirty years before. Huntington has stated they will restore and display the checks. How did the oversight occur? Huntington had acquired over thirty banks so a few details may have been overlooked.

The point is that in Mergers and Deals, things get lost.

Value is an obvious thing that often disappears. A large public company buys a smaller one, for a very big price, based on the smaller one's performance and somehow that valuation never occurs again.

People, lots of people, disappear in Deals. Most buyers have eliminated a competitors' plant and its workers after an acquisition. Management often disappears, too. Within three years, two thirds of an acquired firm's management are gone. Sometimes the secrets to running the business are also gone.

Culture may be the hardest thing to see and quantify, but culture always disappears. The practices and rituals unique to each company are no longer silently passed on to the next generation of employees. Sometimes these are the very things that magically made it work and created value in the first place. When the people and their culture disappear, the value that the buyer thought he bought is gone.

We call this Chapter Mergers and Deals. The bankers' term, Mergers and Acquisitions, has a great ring to it. News stories use the term Merger and public relations people love it.

I will try not to lecture, but be clear on this one thing: "In a Deal, regardless of what it is called, someone bought or took over someone else." One group won and the other lost.

Even if the economics are made to look otherwise. Or, if for some crazy accounting or tax rule, it's called a Merger, it is Not! There are almost no mergers of equals. Banks love to announce and publicly act like everything is equal. Do not believe it. Especially with bankers.

Competitor firms all privately hate each other, at the worst, and are fearful of each other, at the least. So the thing to remember is: in a Deal, someone is bought and someone is sold. Period.

Although this chapter focuses on Deals and their lessons, Mergers and Deals overlap, and connect, through Planning. Deals also tie into Leadership, which ultimately tie into the critical key concept of Culture; these two concepts will follow.

So hang on for Deals!

They are a wild ride that can change your life and stay in your dreams forever.

The Perfect Deal: Donn buys/sells Liskey

Background

As Donn Corp. was becoming the leader in ceiling systems, Don Brown looked for more products he could sell. An emerging business was raised or access floors, which started in computer rooms where all mechanical services were placed under the floor.

Donn moved into the business slowly, buying two small manufacturers for a few million dollars. Sales doubled, then tripled as Donn quickly became the number 3 player.

Then the number 2 player, Liskey, came up for sale. Their owner, a private equity firm, Captech, wanted in today's dollars $10 million, and for Donn to assume the lease on their plant.

Captech was separately negotiating with Liskey's management to buy the business, but they lacked financing.

They also wanted the deal done by yearend- one month away!

Situation Analysis/Strategic Issues of a Liskey Deal

In Deals, like in Planning, we need to look at pros and cons:

Pros:

– Strategic fit with existing Donn floor business

– Liskey brand widely recognized and specified

– Operational fit as both plants were in Baltimore

– Combined sales would equal the market leader, Tate

– Expanding market niche in building materials

– Involved metal processing like Donn ceilings

Cons:

– Major financial investment; Donn's largest deal

– Tight time frame by 12/31 with holidays

– Liskey managers could derail deal or value of combining

– Floors would be secondary to Donn ceilings business

So what to do? The pros were really positive. Donn had enjoyed success and early profits in its flooring business. This seemed like a perfect fit. You could gradually combine operations, sales and management for real synergies and savings. Like many startup businesses, all the plants and people were in one area near Baltimore, Maryland.

The Donn owners and managers decided to proceed.

Due Diligence on Liskey

Have we discussed the concept of Due Diligence yet? In business, and especially Deals, there is nothing more critical. Due Diligence occurs before you sign on the line to buy something. A test drive for a car. Going online before you buy that new big screen television. We all do this, right?

Alas, in Deals, Due Diligence is often overlooked or shortchanged especially by the senior executives of buyers. This is because proper Due Diligence involves detail, can often upset the seller and even kill the Deal, if you discover issues with the target's assets or liabilities. More than that, in our instant world, Due Diligence takes time.

Public sellers like to think all their information is an open book in their SEC filings and Annual Reports. But these documents are much summarized and subject to interpretation, even if audited. Also, often the acquisition target is a smaller part of the public parent. So you must perform Due Diligence.

Private sellers are worse, of course. Founders, especially, feel insulted by a buyer's inquiries. They take it personally.

Liskey was a private subsidiary of the private equity company, Captech. Donn signed a Confidentiality Agreement and a Letter of Intent, subject to Due Diligence. Liskey's management was trying to buy their Company at the same time. We only had a couple of weeks to investigate it before the year-end deadline. This sounded very difficult even under good circumstances and without the insiders bidding. Awkward.

Donn assembled a Team to travel to Baltimore, meet the Liskey managers and start Due Diligence. I was put in charge. We had our experts in credit to look at their receivables. We had manufacturing people to look at their plant, equipment and inventory. Our sales people to review their customer list. My Donn financial friend, Justin, and I covered everything else including taxes, the lease, insurance and, yes, all HR issues. We also had the future issue that when we combined businesses, some managers from Donn or Liskey would lose their jobs.

How to begin our process? A dinner with Liskey!

From Lunches and Dinners, we learned that a social event involving food and wine could help any awkward situation. So a couple of us from Donn's Due Diligence team arrived in time for a dinner that we hoped would include the Liskey managers. This was late December so we were not sure how many would attend. Answer: One of the six invited showed up! Awkward. Gene was the research/technology guy. Very nice but quiet. We explained our interest and our due diligence process. Gene listened.

Later, after meeting all the Liskey team, I concluded they had sent the perfect guy to our dinner. Gene did not know a lot of numbers, or legal things or Deal issues but he really was a great guy and easy to talk with. Would I change and not do the pre-deal dinner again? Never, it is always beneficial. It gave us Donn folk a chance to sell Donn and ourselves in a relaxed setting. We will never know exactly what Gene reported to the other Managers. But

Gene remained with the combined firm until he retired and he and I always had a fun story to tell about how we met. Maybe we created a small bridge to Liskey that evening.

But the next morning it got really awkward when we went to Liskey's offices and met the head financial guy, Jim. He was somehow not available for our dinner and he was not at all thrilled to see anyone trying to buy their company. Jim announced that their President, Ted, was coming back in a day or so, but in the meantime, he was not sure what to provide us or how much to cooperate with us as a competitive bidder. Then an interesting thing occurred. The CFO from the California based parent, Captech, walked in on our meeting with Jim.

None of us were expecting any visitors but this older, to me at the time, CFO, proceeded to explain to Jim that he and the other Liskey Managers were to provide the Donn team with anything they asked for. The CFO further explained that he would hang around for a couple of days to make sure we all got off to a good start. He never needed to inject himself again.

And yes, for the rest of my career, on each Deal, where my company was selling, either I or a very trusted senior person showed up at our local business to make sure the buyer's Due Diligence started out smoothly. Even if the managers in the business you are selling are not bidders, they still can create awkward issues. Issues that can and should be avoided.

The second day of our Due Diligence, Liskey's President, Ted, arrived. He had been in California with Captech trying unsuccessfully, to arrange financing so he and the other Liskey managers could buy the business. When I went to meet him, he was already very unhappy. Awkward. As I walked into his office, he got a phone call, but motioned me to sit down. I did and trying to ignore his call, I looked around the office. There were fascinating black and white photographs decorating the office. My father owned a camera shop so I knew a bit about photography and realized these were not your typical purchased artworks.

When Ted got off the phone, I introduced myself and immediately commented on the black and white photos. I said they had a very personal touch. Ted seemed surprised and stated that yes, he had both taken and enlarged them himself. We talked photography for quite a while. Once we finally got around to business, we both already sensed we might become friends. I was able to assure Ted that we would conduct our process professionally, and that I would meet with him regularly. I also offered to give him insight into the Donn culture that he might be joining. We became and remained lifelong friends.

So what did we learn about Liskey in our Due Diligence?

– Financial results were accurate
– Customer list and margins excellent
– Asset values appropriate and fair
– No significant additional liabilities

That was all very positive news which allowed Donn's planned purchase to proceed. But we also discovered more about Liskey:

– Managers in many functional areas were superior
– Product development was better
– Operating and computer systems were superior

This was all unexpected and a problem. You see, Don Brown had assumed we would just fire all the Liskey managers and have our Donn Floor team run the combined business. Again, Awkward. Knowing Mr. Brown as I did, I chose to avoid bringing this issue up. Instead, I encouraged the other senior Donn executives to visit the Liskey facility, meet their people and look at their processes and systems. It became obvious to everyone. Within a few months of our purchase, all the Liskey managers were running the combined business and several Donn people had departed.

Results of the Liskey Deal

Over the next decade, the combined sales of Donn and Liskey Flooring grew four times. By the time of the Donn sale to USG Corporation, Flooring worldwide accounted for over 25% of Donn's sales. The annual profits alone were more than the total purchase price Donn had paid for Liskey and the earlier businesses. Donn became the U.S. industry leader with over 40% market share and set up successful flooring operations in Canada, Europe, and South Africa. It was a Deal home run!

But few Deals remain perfect forever. Access Flooring use in general offices did occur, but only for a decade. Their initial higher cost of installation troubled many building owners. As computers became smaller and required less care, that market also shrank. Access Flooring is still around today but is used more in specialty applications. One of the last acts I did for USG was to sell Flooring to our major competitor, Tate.

Sale of Donn/USG Interiors Flooring Business

Access Floors had a great run for Donn and for USG Interiors after Donn was acquired. We already covered a mini version of the Situation Analysis/Strategic Issues that led to the decision to sell Flooring. The key positive decision for USG Interiors was recognizing these factors and exiting the business while there was still something to sell. And, in this case, knowing one large, financially able and willing buyer, Tate.

Often, the sale of a business involves our Wizard Bankers and their fees plus an elaborate Selling Memorandum or an auction with buyers from all over the world. None of this occurred.

I called Don, the head guy of Tate's business who I had known for a number of years. We met, alone, no Bankers or Lawyers, and settled on the sales price. We both knew the industry and each other's businesses. And we came up with a mutually acceptable valuation and outlined the key Deal terms.

Sadly, this old, honorable way of deal making has been long gone since the Gordon Gekko code of Greed appeared. Here, two knowledgeable, business principals agreed to the major terms. Then, we got our bankers and lawyers involved to finish up. Nowadays, many principals do not understand their own business. Or they are overly concerned about getting sued by their shareholders. Or their own Lawyers convince them that they cannot possibly negotiate without attorneys being present. But here outside Advisors would add no value. We closed the Deal.

Deal Truisms

The concept of two knowledgeable people who respect each other and get a deal done will lead us to other Deal truisms.

–   It is more fun to buy a company than to sell one. This is true because buying is exciting. It is exciting to the Management team and the Board and often even the Shareholders.

–   It is more fun to do the Deal than do the Due Diligence. Again, Deals are exciting but good diligence involves detail and work. Even Deal contract negotiations can be boring. Private equity firms, however, love all this detail and use it to wear down the corporate people they are Dealing with. This is why large, public firms overpay when buying.

–   Selling is much harder than buying. When you buy, everyone is excited; when you sell, it is because something did not work. The Seller may just want to get rid of a mistake.

–   Big, public companies often pay too much for smaller firms, they also sell businesses for too little. Yes, I am repeating this notion. Again this is especially the case when dealing with private equity firms where another critical factor is that private equity people invest their own money in every Deal. By contrast, most public Managers have very little invested.

–   Watch out for the management team you are selling. Even if your managers are not trying to buy the business, like they were in Donn buying Liskey, they can compromise your Deal unless you manage your people that you are selling.

Both Sides Now: USG Corporation buys Donn Corporation

<u>Personal Background</u>

The Sale of Donn to USG impacted and changed my life more than any other single, career event. Professionally, I moved to a giant, unknown and totally different culture firm. Personally, my wife, Tricia, and I moved to the great city of Chicago.

So sit back and enjoy the story of this fateful Deal, with the unusual title, Both Sides Now, which we will explain later.

As always, we will start with the Strategic Issues.

<u>Situation Analysis/Strategic Issues for Donn:</u>
- Sales of $300 million; 20 global plants
- Leader in ceiling grids; #2 in access floors
- Strong annual compound sales and profit growth
- Finances and debt under control with solid cash flow
- Brown family succession underway, no interest in selling
- Excellent, driven/loyal managers with phantom stock plan

<u>Situation Analysis/Strategic Issues for USG:</u>
- Sales of $3 billion; 200 North America plants
- Leader in gypsum wallboard systems along with other businesses
- Recent record sales and profits
- Viewed by Wall Street as stodgy and conservative
- Mixed to poor history of non-gypsum successes
- Common stock price lags behind other building companies

<u>A study by USG's Strategy VP, formerly of McKinsey, showed:</u>

- o Commercial Interiors as key growth area

- o Ceiling grids needed to complement USG's ceiling tile

- o The preferred acquisition: private firm, Donn

Wow! Is that the recipe for a Deal or a disaster?

<u>The Big Con aspect of Deals</u>

Many times Deals have aspects similar to a con job. In a quarter of all my Deals, one party, usually the seller, makes some outlandish claim. Often, it is about a new secret product they are inventing and this adds a layer of excitement.

So the world of Con artists and the world of Dealmakers have a lot in common. In honor of this, we will use the titles from the big con movie <u>The Sting</u> to analyze this Deal.

<u>The Players</u>

Every Con or Deal has key players and critical roles they perform. In The Sting this is done through an opening con that goes very wrong. But in this Deal we have:

Patriarchs: (like all Generals, best behind the lines)
- – Donn's founder Don Brown, engineer and salesman
- – USG's Chairman/CEO Bob Day, a career salesman

Mediators: (to get and keep the Deal moving)
- – Donn's U.S. President Tom
- – USG's President, Ralph and CFO, Gene

Lead Negotiators: (those into the dirty details)
- – Donn's CFO Brad (me)
- – USG's Strategy group VP Bill and his guy, Len

<u>The Setup</u>

This occurs at the beginning of the Con/Deal and establishes the overall objectives and strategy to be used. In the movie, Redford travels to Chicago to partner with the master Newman. Here, it all started with USG calling on Don Brown and stating their interest. Don Brown had had suitors before. He did not flatly say no! Or yes, either.

Let's start with the pre-negotiating planning. Both sides have to think independently about the key Objectives to be addressed in a potential Deal.

USG Objectives in acquiring Donn:
– Achieve superior growth in a new business, Interiors
– Enhance USG management with the aggressive Donn team
– Pay fairly for Donn value to increase-not dilute-USG stock

Donn Objectives in a sale to USG:
– Money! A premium price for the Brown family
– Protect Donn managers with retention contracts
– Keep Donn intact as a separate USG business

As we look at these Objectives we have conflicts. USG fairly paying for value does not tie into a high price for Don Brown. And how can Donn stay separate and help the new Interiors segment grow? Deal objectives often need to be flexible. Maybe both sides will approach the negotiations in a helpful way?

<u>USG's approach to negotiations:</u>

– Classical cash flow model to determine value and price

– Flexibility in structure due to Donn's private nature

– High road, direct open style; part of USG's culture

<u>Donn's approach to negotiations:</u>

– High demands, low data, secretive, Russian style

Well, this is going to be a challenge to get done!

The initial negotiating sessions reflected the vast differences between the two sides as to their respective views on price and their approach to the whole process.

But before we started negotiating, Donn hired two advisors. Smith Barney, who created a financial valuation on what the Browns could receive if we did a management buyout versus a sale. Their range of values were $80 to $120 million. Smith Barney wanted to lead our Deal team but we said no because we wanted to control the Deal not leave it to a fee driven Advisor.

Then we hired McKinsey. We knew that USG had just hired their Strategy VP, Bill, from McKinsey. We also knew Donn needed help presenting its uniqueness to the much larger firm.

The negotiations began. USG provided us with a 50-page packet that discussed their overall corporate strategy, focus on Interiors, what a great fit Donn would be, and the shareholder equity value model (Alcar) they were using to evaluate us. All of this was very confidential and yet very useful to us. We provided

USG with a half dozen pieces of paper with consolidated financial information and a two-year forecast. All very top of the pile. Interesting but not real helpful. We were private.

Shortly into the Setup phase we get to price.

USG offers us $85 million. Our response goes like this.

– Brad to Brown: This is great! We have done zero and they are close to our banker's price range!
– Brown to Brad: Ask them for $175 million.
– Brad protesting: But that could scare them away!
– Brown calmly: Ask for $175 million.

The Deal dies the first time. But we agree to reveal more of our secrets in a one time, special meeting only for USG.

The Hook

Now in The Sting this is where a fake drunk Paul Newman takes bad guy, Robert Shaw's, money in a rigged poker game. Shaw "accidentally" meets Robert Redford who claims to hate Newman and the plot for revenge moves ahead.

What Don Brown dreamed up was a bit different but it had aspects of a carnival where con artists work their magic. We rented a warehouse near our Ohio headquarters and set up a Product Fair. This became a limited use place to display all our flashier products and to display behind special curtains, some new secret products. This was only if Mr. Brown decided USG seemed worthy and interested. And we told USG, no price discussions would be covered, just Donn's philosophy.

We invite only USG's senior team and, we insist this must be done on a Sunday afternoon in December to avoid any watchful eyes. All of this mystery to make Donn seem even more desirable.

Somehow, USG actually came and the carnival began:

- Don Brown spoke of his philosophy on selecting, rewarding and managing people. He never stuck to any script; he just talked.
- Tom spoke about Donn's people, markets and our propensity for action and results. The highlight was a 30-year timeline chart that showed Donn's new products, international or acquisition expansion and sales growth to $300 million. Quite a story.
- Then, as in any good carnival or fair, a surprise guest! McKinsey. They gave a wonderful McKinsey presentation complete with elaborate charts. It covered three areas: Donn's Management Philosophy, its Strategic Positions, and our View on Value.
- Then we toured the Product Fair, which was also impressive.
- Don Brown did reveal the new secret products. Mr. Brown suggested that these two secret items could be worth hundreds of millions of additional profits for a Donn/USG combination. Wow!
- The Product Fair and the presentation talks were a huge success and certainly provided The Hook.

<u>The Tale</u>

In a big con, this is where all the parts of the hoax come together. In The Sting, Newman and Redford recruit an army of con artists as Redford shows Shaw how they will bankrupt Newman's betting parlor using The Wire.

For Donn and USG the equivalent was getting into more details and doing due diligence on each other. For Donn, we had to find a way to increase USG's sense of our value thus the price for our business. We did this in two ways. We bought the ALCAR valuation model that USG was using. With the help of McKinsey and Smith Barney we learned to modify our Donn forecasts to show more value. We also added back to the historical Donn financial results the Brown family costs and adjusted for accounting/tax practices that would not occur in a public company. Profits and price up!

Meanwhile USG was also studying Donn. They looked at our limited public filings and credit reports. They also were allowed to do a secret tour of our main Ohio plant.

Then we had another meeting on Value and Purchase Price.

USG, after studying our new numbers, offers $125 million

- Brad to Don Brown: This is really great! This is way above our banker's range. We should move our $175 million down and get this done!
- Brown to Brad: Tell them I want $175 million

The Deal dies a 2nd time.

USG suggests their Chairman Bob Day meet alone with our Don Brown. I tell my USG friends that this is a bad idea.

The Deal dies a 3rd time. Well, we know how this ends.

The Sting or the Finale

In the movie, Shaw places a huge bet in Newman's place but the information is wrong. As he protests that he is losing a fortune, the FBI busts in and shoots Newman and Redford dead.

But this is not Butch Cassidy and the Sundance Kid! The FBI are part of the con! Everyone lives and is happy, except the bad guy Shaw, who flees without his money, from the fake FBI!

The Sting is complete; revenge and money are sweet.

Our bankers, Smith Barney, suggest maybe it's time for a third party, like them, to try to help. Out of frustration, exhaustion and some desperation, both sides agree. Another dreaded meeting on price is set at USG's Chicago offices.

We convince Mr. Brown to stay in a hotel room nearby. USG makes their Chairman Bob stay out of sight.

– We make a Deal at $140 million
– The Deal is completed 9 months after the first casual meeting with Don Brown. Not an unusual timeframe.
– All the Brown family exit the company and sell their stock
– The Donn managers are protected with three year contracts
– Donn, for one year, remains separate within USG Interiors

Results of USG Acquiring Donn:

The combined Donn/Interior group in its first 3 years:

– Sales up 27% and earnings up 57%

– The organizational fit was much harder. Many of the Donn managers refused to move to Chicago and work for the much larger, very differently styled company. Many of their USG peers in Interiors retire. The new Interiors unit in its first several years had two CEOs, two Chief Operating Officers, two H.R. Vice Presidents and several different structures. A ton of industry knowledge was lost.

Long term, today the Interiors business of USG is one of three core USG businesses. In this latest economic downturn, as in past U.S. building recessions, Donn and Interiors have been the main profitable part of USG Corporation. Go Figure!

Truisms/Lessons We can Learn from Donn/USG

– Be patient in Deal making. Or, in Deal vernacular, every Deal must die or go into the toilet several times.

– Be careful how you negotiate/balance your motives. USG was too open and direct with Donn. Likewise, Donn was secretive and slow in revealing needed data.

– Manage who negotiates and when. The Donn and USG Chairmen were well meaning but accomplished nothing. The Donn bankers in the end, brokered the Deal.

– Again, big public companies often pay more than they have to for private firms. Real synergies like combining ceiling tile and grid products create shareholder value. Bringing in new managers to change culture often does not.

– Finally the title of this Deal, Both Sides Now. After the Deal was completed USG's Strategy VP, Bill, moved to operations with our new Interiors group and USG promoted me to Strategy VP. About that time, Bill and I gave a joint speech about the Donn/USG Deal to several national, financial strategy groups. We called it Both Sides Now since:

1. We used two facing podiums and took turns detailing each of our thought process and actions.

2. I had switched sides and moved into Bill's job of strategy at USG; a major change from the world of Donn.

Both Sides Now, the Deal of my business career.

Lessons Learned from Mergers and Deals

A lot is lost in Mergers and Deals: People, Value and Culture.

The Term "Merger" is misused. Someone bought someone. There are no mergers of equals. Someone won, someone lost.

Even an initially perfect Deal, like Donn buys Liskey, has a timeframe or life and then you need to exit.

In an acquisition, do a Situation Analysis of the pros and cons.

Relationships in Deals can start hostile but end up friendly.

Having two parties who respect and trust each other negotiate without Advisors is always best.

It is more fun to buy a company than to sell one.

It is more fun to do the Deal than do due diligence.

Big, public firms often pay too much for smaller firms and they also sell these businesses for too little.

Watch out for the Management Team you are selling; they can move too quickly to help the buyer not you.

Deals have many aspects of big cons, so be watchful.

Be patient in Deal making. Deals often die three times.

Be careful how you negotiate and try to balance your motives of maximizing price versus getting the Deal done.

Manage who negotiates and when. Avoid Chairmen and Owners.

Sometimes in Deals, business or life, you can end up on both sides of the Deal of your lifetime. Enjoy it!

13. Culture and Leadership
(The Flip side of Each Other)

Overview

Over the last several decades, many famous management writers, have cited the clear linkage between Culture and Leadership. Leaders, especially founders, create the early Culture of a firm with the first rules, standards of performance and values. Like Apple's founder, Steve Jobs, and his passion for design and operational excellence. Founders can be hard acts to follow. Subsequent Leaders can either destroy a Culture or dramatically refocus it. The recent revolving Leaders at Hewlett-Packard have changed strategies so often, it's hard to identify the core values and Culture established by its founders. So, for good or bad, Leaders greatly impact their company's Culture.

Similarly, a firmly entrenched Culture often molds and chooses the Leaders who will best represent and maintain its specific values and traditions, hence, the frequent announcement that a company is promoting a long time insider to take over as CEO. When an outsider sneaks in at the top, they often fail because they did not respect the Culture.

So Culture can impact and change Leaders just like Leaders can impact and change Culture. Or, as famous writers, long before me, have stated, Culture and Leadership are the flip side of each other- like the flip side of the same coin.

Everyone knows that Leadership is important whether it's to run governments, businesses, or sports. The media is constantly criticizing leaders. Professional coaches come to mind. By contrast, Cultures are more complex, harder to define and challenge. By refusing to accept Walmart as a threat to its huge retail business, Sears thought they would go on forever but they were wrong. Because of Culture and Leadership, organizations either thrive and grow, or shrink and wither away; these are the two most powerful principles to understand and master if you want to succeed in any career.

In fact, Culture and Leadership are the keys to group and individual success, everywhere. In many ways, everything we have covered so far fits into one of these. As always, we compare and contrast some real life examples to show how and when some things worked well and not so well. Perhaps we will even flip back and forth. So pay attention!

A Historical look at Culture-the Royal B.C. Museum

In Victoria, Canada, the Museum has a wing dedicated to their aboriginal founders called the First People's Exhibit.

As you enter you are greeted with this quote:

"Environment and Culture: In order to survive, humans must provide for their material, emotional and intellectual needs. These are satisfied by Culture, a complex system that includes tools, language, arts and beliefs. And Cultures can vary because they must be compatible with their supporting environments."

This statement can describe Culture in any organization:

- Culture satisfies needs critical to survival; firms provide both monetary and social rewards to those who embrace the Culture and fires those who do not "fit."
- Culture is a complex system of language, tools and beliefs. Organizations have their own sets of unique words, procedures, forms and verbal histories.
- Cultures must be compatible with the environment. Rapid growth requires different beliefs and tools vs. slow or no growth. For example, when companies slow down after decades of growth, they often perish.

So let's remember this quote as we move forward.

A Historical look at Leadership-the German Military

This story is attributed to my old USG CEO, Gene. He had served in the Navy and enjoyed military analogies. Whether it's fully historically accurate or not, this is a fascinating take on Leadership from Gene, a great leader, mentor, and friend.

During the Second World War, the German military used extensive personality tests. They came up with a four-box matrix to categorize their recruits, and help predict their advancement potential, and future rank in the service.

The complete matrix as shown on the following page:

- Work ethic down the vertical: (Lazy to Ambitious)
- Intelligence along the horizontal axis

	Little Intelligence	**Very Intelligent**
L		
A		
Z	Privates	Generals
Y		
A		
M		
B		
I		
T	Sergeants	Lieutenants/Majors
I		
O		
U		
S		

Now I know you are thinking that I made a mistake! The Generals cannot be very intelligent and very lazy. How can they be Generals? Well! Let's start at the bottom with Privates and work up. Our army titles really apply to all organizations whether in government, not for profits or the corporate world.

Privates: They are at the bottom. That said, this matrix is not about where you start but a predictor of where you could end up. Everyone starts out low. Some have more smarts and drive and move up. But those with little intelligence or ambition are doomed to remain as Privates. In the corporate world, the equivalent would be entry-level office or factory jobs. You do not count on this group to come up with a lot of new ideas, or initiatives and you really do not expect or want them to.

Sergeants: This group lacks a lot of intelligence but they are hard working. You give them an order and they will get it done. Round up the Privates and charge up a hill facing death; Yes Sir! They do not come up with a lot of their own ideas. In the business world, this group might include office managers and factory foremen. Nothing gets done without good Sergeants.

Lieutenants/Majors: This group is considered both intelligent and ambitious. Those who graduate from officer training schools or West Point are immediately Lieutenants and can move up to Major. This group helps to create strategy and execute it, since they are very close to the battle lines.

In the Vietnam War, the life expectancy of a newly landed 2nd Lieutenant is quoted as 16 combat minutes. In the corporate world, career survival is often only slightly longer. The equivalent job titles, can be Senior Manager, Director or even Vice President. In the ever increasing world of corporate downsizing, these jobs are often eliminated when departments are combined. And this group, whether in the military or in business, can provide wonderful scapegoats to take the blame for a failed project or initiative. After all they were technically in charge or on the steering committee or something. This protects the Generals from getting their hands dirty.

Generals: We're finally full circle. We can all see that Generals must be very intelligent. But why should these smart, high potential, possible future Generals be lazy? They need to be lazy, so they do not micro-manage and try to do everything themselves. After all they have staff! They have the Lieutenants and Majors to take their brilliant ideas and tweak them so they are practical and may actually work. And they have scores of hard working Sergeants to grind things out with the Privates. What Generals, like our outlaw friend Butch Cassidy, are good at is thinking! That is why they are, at their best, a bit lazy.

We have had some U.S. Presidents, like Jimmy Carter, who were very brilliant people but were thought to over-manage or refuse to delegate. His successor, President Ronald Reagan, may not have been lazy but he certainly presented a much more relaxed public profile. Reagan is ranked much more successful.

In the corporate world, the equivalent of General is, President or CEO. And, yes, they are best, if a bit lazy.

My old friend and USG boss, Gene, had all those titles. When I asked him, if he thought he was lazy, he just smiled.

So this got me to thinking.

When USG Corporation went through its first Financial Crisis and bankruptcy, I wrote how our core Crisis team worked seven 10-hour days a week forever. Gene never told me to do that. We just did it. When we needed Gene by phone at 9 pm on a weeknight or on the weekend, we found him. If we needed him to meet some banker or lawyer and wave the senior corporate flag, he was there. But Gene let us, his Crisis team, his Lieutenants and Majors, plot most of the strategy and do most of the negotiating for days on end.

We understood, (and he made sure we did), what was important to him and we stayed in constant contact with Gene on these matters. But the bulk of the deal was the Crisis team's deal. Sure, as CEO/Chairman of the Board, Gene and the whole Board had to formally vote and approve our final plan, but Gene knew how to pick good people, delegate huge responsibilities to them, and then stay out of their way and away from the details.

Gene was not lazy. He was a great General. And a great Leader. And he could tell great stories!

Culture and Leadership at Donn Corporation

One Half of a Two-Car Garage:

The story of Donn starts like a lot of startups, in a garage. The founding of Apple Computer and a number of other famous firms often began in a setting like this one.

Don Brown also left a job as an engineer to start Donn just as he and his wife were starting a family. A big risk.

Don Brown, Founder and Leader:

We have talked a lot about Don Brown. We learned he was a super salesman in selling a modular hotel to the giant Holiday Inn. We learned that he created unique rewards, like the Christmas gifts for all employees' children and without help or hindrance from any Human Resource minions. We even learned that sometimes the freedom he gave his managers and how his lack of controls could lead to management fraud. But let's take a more structured look at Mr. Brown as a Leader.

Brown's Overall Strategic Vision

Don Brown always said he wanted to build an American enterprise. He believed in the American Dream that said hard work would lead to success. He also wanted something that would provide lasting value for the country. In addition, he never had a clear idea of what his next product innovation would be but he knew his team would figure it out.

Donn's product innovations started with commercial ceilings. Over the thirty years he owned Donn, the company introduced over twenty new products for commercial buildings. Some, like the modular buildings, were never the success he hoped for. Some came from acquiring new companies, like Liskey and their access floors. But what Don Brown really stressed was that you had to keep coming up with new things.

He also always wanted to be first with every new product or service. Donn started computer aided design services for their customers to help layout a building's ceilings, walls and floors. Donn was also the first in its industry to go international, as we have discussed.

So Don Brown's overall strategic vision was this: Be first to create new building material products and services in new global marketplaces to keep the Company growing. And how did he execute this? Through people.

Brown's Approach to People

In Hiring: Don Brown looked for people who were, like him, driven, intelligent and loyal. The driven or ambitious trait made the workplace more challenging and interesting. And with the constant growth, there were new job opportunities to fill. The intelligence was needed to make and rapidly execute his ever-changing plans. Without a lot of staff, everyone had to be mentally able and motivated enough to make decisions. In addition, loyalty was critical. He also liked to have potential long-timers who could grow with his growing company. He also liked them because he, like many self-made entrepreneurs, was extremely concerned about confidentiality in all matters. Donn was a very private firm with loyal, tight-lipped people.

In Career Advancement: Don Brown managed to convince all of his employees that there was no better place to work. This feeling was shared from the plant floor to the small executive office. Brown talked nonstop about the future growth of the company and thus your own individual growth as well. He believed that the Company and his people had no boundaries in products, markets or geography. Ceiling salesmen became general managers in our smaller businesses. In fact, many of our managers believed they would become or retire as millionaires, because Don Brown repeatedly told them that they would. The world was our oyster, because we worked for Don Brown. This created a strong esprit de corps. We were all considered special and privileged. After Donn was sold to USG, a number of senior people retired young or started non-business careers, in part, because they believed they would not be able to experience the unique culture of Donn anywhere else.

In Career Demotions: This may sound odd but it was another skill Don Brown had that many larger firms lack. As Donn grew,

Mr. Brown knew he needed different types of managers with different skills. But instead of discarding the former managers, he somehow created new roles for them which gave them dignity and respect. The first head of engineering, George, stayed with Donn for forty years even after he was gradually moved several levels down the official organization chart. The first Treasurer, Joe, became the head of purchasing before he retired.

Don Brown managed to do this demoting smoothly by being open with the people, by leaving their old salaries in place and by personally staying in touch with them on certain matters. It was as if their importance, at least to him, had not changed. He demanded loyalty from his people but he gave it back. Most large companies fail miserably when dealing in this area.

In Summation. Don Brown often stated that since he was not a very good manager, he had to work hard to surround himself with only very good managers. Like a great General with his staff in this case.

That is Leadership. And that translates to Culture, because Culture is the flip side of Leadership.

Culture at Donn Corporation

Here I will use some of the materials we and our advisor, McKinsey, provided to USG Corporation as part of the sale process. This became a large part of the limited written summary of Donn's unique Culture. Let's take a look.

Entrepreneurship: Donn operated in a very loose manner. It was as if each staff or operating group was on its own.

In Don Brown's office was a twisted, deformed, early ceiling grid prototype that went off in every direction. Everyone said that was how Don Brown looked at the organization. No real recognizable structure. So people operated as if they were running their own group or business. You hired and fired people with very few guidelines. Compensation usually exceeded that of both Donn's competitors and larger firms like USG. The ownership idea was strengthened initially with minority stock and later a phantom stock plan for senior managers. You knew that the Brown family owned the company but somehow you felt it was partially yours, so you treated the company with respect.

Innovation: This went far beyond new product or engineering processes. We had a company-wide voicemail system before the larger firms. Innovation at Donn took more of a "just get it done" approach. Staff and operating groups could experiment with new equipment or software or even hire those dreaded outside advisors, if you could make things work better. It was a Culture that let you push the boundaries of your group until you bumped into another Donn group and then you talked about it.

Donn was also the first in the building industry to use customer incentive trips to Russia or Hong Kong. Then there was a company yacht Caranita, in the Bahamas. At Donn, unlike so many firms today, you were expected to be pushy and innovative and if something failed that was ok. And you did not have to fill out elaborate proposal forms with five layers of approval or beat phony cost of capital hurdles to get things done. And innovation was tied to ownership, and to entrepreneurship.

Why don't more companies encourage and promote these qualities in their people and their culture? At Donn, growth in sales was the priority. Profits were secondary. We had to be willing to wait for financial results and higher profits, which usually followed. In a way this is like many tech startups, (think Twitter or Facebook), who focus solely on growth in website hits then later on cash flow and profits.

By contrast, most established public firms focus almost exclusively on earnings per share, quarter by quarter. This is what Wall Street analysts and, often sadly, the companies own short-sighted stockholders fixate on. At the end of the day, all businesses, even private or tech ones, need to make money. Or they really are not a viable business. But private firms, like Donn, can focus on what they want as long as they are private.

Minimal Bureaucracy and Hierarchy: Donn had a very limited headquarters staff. There were not many formal systems or procedures of any kind. Again, this lack of formal structure goes along with Donn's focus on ownership and innovation. Remember the opening quote about Canada's ancient First People: the culture must fit within and be supported by the environment. Don Brown led and operated in a free and loose style; thus Donn's Leadership and the Culture had to be compatible.

An Oral, not Written Culture: This may sound odd but it was true. Donn's management style was very verbal, either on the phone, on voicemail or face-to-face. When USG acquired Donn, they emphasized, this difference in a newsletter, since USG was very much a written culture. For Donn, the oral aspect goes back, like many things, to Don Brown; he hated to read! That is why Donn was a beta test site for an early voicemail system.

Don Brown was oral, not written, and thus the company he founded was oral. Remember the weekly taped messages that the managers submitted in exchange for cash? Oral. Donn also had a lot of face-to-face meetings. Staff meetings. Senior managers meetings. Sales meetings. My own worldwide Controller meetings. Before people wrote articles and books about management by walking around or traveling around, Donn was doing just that. It makes a huge difference to actually meet someone in person, especially at our endless Donn lunches and dinners. Business became much easier.

That's why, oral beats written every time.

Respect, Trust and Faith in Individuals: This last aspect of Donn's Culture is, in a way, a summation of all the other traits. Our Canadian SuperMarketer, Frank, recently reminded me of this. He said that at Donn, you were given respect and trust on day one. Respect, for the background you brought to Donn from the outside. Trust, to make decisions and to create new initiatives. Faith that you would deal fairly with people. You were treated with respect, until you lost people's trust. This is very different from most firms.

Usually, you have to earn people's trust and respect. Sometimes by just putting in time. Sometimes by not breaking the rules or complaining. And sometimes, by actually doing something worthy of others' respect and trust. If a company strives to create a sense of ownership and encourages the pursuit of innovation in a loosely structured, oral world, you better have respect, trust and faith in people or you are not going to get far.

We all learned that from Mr. Brown and tried to treat each other in a respectful, trusting way.

Culture and Leadership at USG Corporation

In a rare, company issued book, commemorating USG's first 50 years, the first words were "Before the dawn of recorded history, a mineral was created...Gypsum." In company videos, these words are often accompanied by pictures of gypsum crystals or a gypsum ore boat coming out of the Canadian mist.

USG, originally called United States Gypsum Company, considers itself to have both a sense of longevity and a special tie to the earth. Much of this relates to the gypsum mineral.

Plaster, made of gypsum, has been used in construction back to Egypt and the pyramids. That is a lot of longevity.

And USG Corporation is a 100-year-old company with some interesting leaders and culture of its own.

Leaders at USG Corporation

For a firm that has been around over 110 years, USG has had only eight Chairman/CEOs-and only three in its first 90+ years. The average CEO tenure today is eight years. The longevity of USG's leaders also had a profound effect forming its culture.

Sewell Avery: If USG had an entrepreneurial era it was all due to this man. Avery was in charge from the founding through the first 50 years! The company rose from inception to over $250 million in sales. Avery acquired and integrated dozens of small gypsum companies and created United States Gypsum. Although he was a risk taker on acquisitions, he was also a financial conservative. Most of the deals were for the new USG stock. Sales and profits all came from gypsum, called the "white dust."

In their first 50 years, USG boasted of only having to borrow money twice! The company, under Avery's tight cost controls, made money and paid dividends every year even during the great Depression! A far cry from what has happened in recent decades. The business writer, Jim Grant, once wrote that poor Sewell must be rolling over in his grave!

At the same time, Sewell Avery also managed to be the CEO of retailer Montgomery Ward. A true captain of industry.

So how do you replace a legend like Avery?

With a guy named Tex.

Tex Shaver: USG's second Chairman was a former CPA who Avery had hired. Tex was in charge for 25 years, which we might call the caretaker era or the first professional management period of USG. Sales were essentially flat growing from $250 million to $300 million with only five acquisitions. Gypsum products were still the story but had been reduced to 60% of sales and 70% of profits. A Fortune magazine article titled "No Nonsense" pretty much tells the story. Tex was quoted as saying that USG was well positioned with its "conservative financial resources; low cost, quality products and its closely guarded industry leadership position." The article concludes that USG was "preoccupied with cost control, and not interested in any business with complicated manufacturing processes." The company's "trademark was independence" as a result of little competition, no unions, steady dividends, and no outside bankers. Those were the days!

How do you or do you want to replace this guy?

<u>Graham Morgan:</u> USG promoted a mid-40's career salesman to be their third Chairman/CEO and he remained in charge for almost twenty years. There were two very distinct strategic eras that occurred under Morgan. The beginning of his tenure could be called aggressive diversification. Morgan made almost 20 acquisitions, many a long way from the old core gypsum. The new businesses ranged from real estate development and home construction to building materials like carpet, metal doors, shower enclosures and a brick refractory. Sales went from $300 million to $1.5 billion and at one point, gypsum products were under 30% of the total. And that's not all!

To manage his diverse company, Morgan moved from USG's functional, centralized management structure to a decentralized form with heads of each business group and even a first time head of international. The physical embodiment of all this change was a newly built, company owned headquarters in downtown Chicago, started by Tex but with Morgan, as its driving force.

The Company wrote that the new building was: bold but conservative, a silent witness to character and purpose and used natural materials from the same good earth as gypsum. For any major company, building a new headquarters is a major event and an ego trip for its sponsor.

Somehow both time and culture seemed to freeze for awhile for USG with its first ever, new building.

The second strategic era for Morgan involved the first outside threat USG had ever really encountered. The U.S. government began a decade long, antitrust review and trial of the gypsum industry for price fixing. USG the company, a number of its officers, and several competitors all pleaded "no contest" and paid millions of dollars in fines. The impact of this on an old-fashioned firm like USG was devastating. This began USG's cultural and organizational retrenchment era.

Many of the acquired businesses and companies were sold. The management retreated to the comfort of centralization with strong functional heads like purchasing, finance, sales, and manufacturing. And Gypsum moved back up to over 50% of sales. All employees had to read and sign a new legal group booklet, "Corporate Policy and the Law" on things you could not do or even think of doing. Morgan retired and USG's first, bold experiment to diversify and decentralize ended.

Leadership vs. Culture

If children's first five to eight years are the most formative for their personality and future success, what about companies? Well, for USG Corporation, the first three leaders and their 90+ years in charge certainly did a lot to form the initial and ongoing company Culture. One cannot help but wonder if USG and Morgan had not been involved with the anti-trust issues, what might have occurred. The history of companies, like nations, often hinge on some specific, but unforeseen, externally driven event. Morgan obviously had a different vision for the company than his predecessors and he tried to remake it product-wise, management structure-wise and style-wise. But this is also where the debate on leaders versus culture comes in.

Was USG already so entrenched, culturally, as a one product, gypsum company that even someone as strong willed and bold as Morgan could never change it? If not anti-trust, would the next recession have ruined his plans? Could the single minded, low cost, mass production, commodity gypsum people adapt to run a true construction and real estate conglomerate? Would his own chosen successor continue his vision or change it?

So what did his successors do?!!

Subsequent USG Chairmen Leaders

We have already written a bit about those who followed Graham Morgan. Having worked with most of them, they are individually and collectively a fine group of leaders. But a very strange thing seemed to happen to those at the top of USG. Like Morgan, they all started a growth plan sometimes even investing outside of gypsum, but, almost always, another outside event or crisis occurred which took years and millions to billions to fix.

In The USG Financial Crisis, we covered how two Chairmen, Bob Day and Gene Connolly, had to deal with the cost of fixing the company and its financial structure while defending the firm from hostile takeovers.

Bill Foote, who followed Gene Connolly, spent about as much time and even more corporate funds to eliminate the asbestos threat that led to USG's second bankruptcy.

Expansion and growth are sacrificed when you don't know if your company will even survive.

Perhaps the current Chairman, Jim Metcalf, will be able to break this cycle and return USG to some of its earlier growth.

That said, let's turn from USG leadership and look at its flip side, culture.

Culture at USG Corporation

As mentioned, leadership often forms the culture and vice versa. We have just talked about some very forceful yet different leaders during USG's formative years.

Remember the Canadian First Nations quote? "Culture is a complex system that involves tools, arts and beliefs." The business writer Edgar Schein called this "levels of culture" which we will use to look at USG.

Artifacts and Creations: This is the first layer of culture. For a 100-year-old company, there was little officially written about USG. But since 1905, the Company has published and given away tens of thousands of copies of a book called, The Gypsum Construction Handbook. It explains how to plan and install building products and systems. Every architect, contractor and journeyman carpenter has one. It is considered a bible, of sorts, for basic interior construction and the Handbook is free. Sure it is part advertising, but it's more a technical guide than a sales brochure. To USG, the Handbook is their responsibility and duty.

Values: This is the second level or layer of culture. Values are ingrained in an organization and its people. They can become a great source of strength. For USG, the first value was honesty and integrity in all dealings from internal to external. Obviously, this core value was severely strained with the price-fixing action. The

239

second value is that USG operates in a highly disciplined, cost efficient manner. This value goes back to the one gypsum product and the centralized functional bureaucracy it allowed. This no frills approach even extends to sales and marketing (versus Donn's lavish customer trips).

The third value is a focus on quality products and services. To this day, when you ask a local drywall installer which manufacturer's "mud" or drywall compound they prefer, it's always USG: it's consistent!

The fourth value is worker and product safety. At USG, safety from the mines to the plants to the distribution business is a type of religion that many other firms should emulate.

USG's final Value is a desire for a conservative financial position. This may go back to Sewell Avery but in a cyclical business like construction it is very fitting and logical. The problem for USG is that their various financial crises caused by hostile takeovers or asbestos litigation have repeatedly pushed this Value into another dimension.

Basic Assumptions: This is how an organization views reality and how it relates to its environment. These characteristics are almost invisible and often taken for granted, but they can impact everything.

At USG, the first basic assumption, not surprisingly, is the firm's "relation to the good earth." When longtime officers and key managers retire, they are given "a piece of the rock," a chunk of crystalized gypsum. It follows you into retirement.

The second basic assumption is continuity with the past, in other words, longevity. It may relate to gypsum's own long history or to the Company's hundred plus years. Either way, at USG, longevity ties to "independence". The gypsum business was, at best, an oligopoly with very few competitors. The company historically had no unions and little debt or reliance on the world of Wall Street. All of this was shattered in the last couple decades with the two bankruptcies and the asbestos issue.

The final basic assumption or internal reality at USG is to be consistent and uniform in how the company operates. Again, the idea of a mass-produced, product like gypsum wallboard certainly lends itself to this concept. Attempts to diversify away from gypsum might have led to incompatible cultures that might have resulted in failures.

Summing up USG's Leadership and Culture

My old MBA professor, Suresh Srivastva, wrote that the real challenge for leaders is to balance or blend three required ingredients for their organization. Continuity, or maintaining a stable and secure culture. Transition, which involves managing planned change in a shared fashion. Novelty, to create innovation and capture collective spirit.

Avery's startup had novelty and transition that later led to continuity. Shaver's caretaker era had continuity as the company adjusted to the post-WWII period. Morgan started with transition and novelty in the business mix, but by the end, things got back to the continuity of gypsum as new businesses were sold off. Morgan's final novelty was unwanted litigation.

The subsequent leaders all tried some transition and novelty in new businesses. But ultimately, it was the continuity of gypsum that survived, that made enough money to pay off hostile takeovers and asbestos litigation and keep the place going.

So, for me, after looking at USG, its Leaders and Culture from both sides now (inside the place and outside), what is wrong with being just a Gypsum company? Nothing!

Just as long as you are the best Gypsum company on the whole good earth!

How can you benefit from understanding Culture and Leadership?

OK, you're saying, I get it Leadership and Culture are important. But from a personal aspect, how can I benefit?

I'm really glad you asked this one. Let's look at what I tried to do about culture and leadership when Donn was acquired by USG. Initially USG said that all of us Donn managers would stay in Ohio. So I enrolled in a two year Executive MBA program at Case Western. I had always wanted to try this, and the timing given this major transition and my age of 40, seemed like a great fit and maybe helpful in my uncertain future career.

One year into the two year MBA program, USG decides all the senior Donn people have to move to Chicago or die, so to speak. Most of the senior Donn managers did not make the move.

We obviously chose to move, but here is a lesser-known fact. For my final course work at Case, I chose to do a combined study of Culture and Leadership of USG. Some of my new USG bosses let me dig through old files and even interview them. Some of what you read is from that class project (for which I earned an A).

But the point is this, when I arrived at my new job and my new place of work in Chicago, I knew more about USG, its history, its leaders, its values, than a lot of longtime USG people. Did this give me an edge or at least a framework to understand some of the changes and issues USG and I faced going forward?

I am sure it did.

Everyone is not smart or lucky enough to be able to do this. But I truly believe people should try to learn about their new employer. And not just its financial condition, but who their leaders are and what is important in their culture.

As young people move up in their career and look to change jobs, this is even more important. As this chapter illustrated, there are many styles of leadership and many unique aspects of any organization's culture. When you are just starting out it may be easier for you to adapt, but as you become more senior, there are both leaders and cultures you can thrive with and others where you will not be able to succeed.

You may also learn that the firm you are looking at is going through a major crisis or that a new CEO has just arrived and may want to make other changes. All these factors are critical as you look to make a significant job change.

So take time to look hard at both sides of this coin of Culture and Leadership at your prospective new employer before you make that big career move!

The Business Circle and Culture and Leadership

By now you have seen the clear link between Culture and Leadership and their dual importance to a company and to its people. These two factors drive firms and individuals to great success or to dismal failures and often in years not decades.

But the less apparent link is that Culture and Leadership, together or separately tie to everything in an organization and thus everything we have discussed in this book.

For example, Crisis Management reflects how leaders react and also is set within the cultural parameters of a firm. In Management Fraud, we mentioned how the lax Donn culture contributed to the problems, and how some leaders often looked the other way or did not supervise their people properly.

Human Resources reflected a leader like Don Brown and his Company's free flowing style versus a much more controlled approach at USG (my missing aquarium!). International business was also driven by Don Brown or curtained at USG by its leaders or the multiple cultural crises they encountered.

This flows from Planning into Mergers and Deals and essentially everything we have discussed over these pages.

So, Business may be a Zoo but it is also a giant circle of people and a firm's traits and style that are captured in their Culture and Leadership.

Lessons Learned from Culture and Leadership

Culture and Leadership are the flip side of each other:
- Founders/Leaders form or transform Culture
- Culture can chose, form or reject Leaders

Culture and Leadership are the two most powerful aspects of any organization, so understand and master them.

Culture can be defined as a complex system of tools and beliefs.

In the German Military and in most organizations we have:
- Privates who lack drive and smarts
- Sergeants who may not be bright but get things done
- Lieutenants/Majors who can adjust and direct strategy
- Generals who have big visions but let others do the work
- A really good General picks great people, gives them broad directives and gets out of their way

Don Brown's strategic vision of innovation and growth still has a lot of value for many businesses today.

Be Creative with your people on: hiring, career advancement, compensation and rewards and even career demotions.

The best managers/leaders hire really good managers/leaders.

A Culture that revolves around, entrepreneurship, innovation, minimal bureaucracy and is oral can go a long way, fast!

Respect, trust and faith in individuals can still exist in large organizations if the leaders practice these traits.

Companies with a only few leaders over decades can form strong and long lasting cultures, that are not easy to change.

We can study levels of culture like artifacts and core values.

A major challenge for leaders may be to balance these three needed ingredients of their firm's culture:
– Continuity, a stable and secure culture
– Transition, managing change in a shared way
– Novelty, creating innovation and group spirit

In Conclusion: if you want to succeed in any organization you need to study its Leadership and Culture; and at first, adapt or at least respect it, until you get to a position where you can change it or at least try. Good Luck!

The Business Zoo

Epilogue

Flying with Falcons

One of my favorite sports is Falconry. Once this was only available to ancient Kings and their Wizards. But if you ever travel near the border of West Virginia and Virginia, you can participate as well. Two legendary resorts, The Greenbrier and The Homestead will teach you this 4,000-year-old sport. They raise and fly birds of prey-Falcons, Hawks and Owls. Just being able to get up close and personal with these magnificent creatures is a joy. And having one take off and land on your arm, in the intermediate level lesson, is a thrill not easily replicated. With their long, pointed beaks and sharp talons sitting a few inches from your face, it is also intimidating.

On a recent trip to the Homestead we met a wonderful, young Falconer. It was a quiet afternoon in the Falcon business so we were able to meet a number of her birds. After explaining that I had done this before, we were off to the woods with a Harris Hawk. As a student of both animals and people, I asked the Falconer how she decides if someone is actually able to handle, let alone fly, one of her impressive Birds of Prey.

- Falconer: It is a judgment call for sure. You want people who respect the Birds and their power. They are not tame.
- Brad: I should say not. I am not going to try to pet one!
- Falconer: Even after I warn people, some try to touch them. One lady tried to kiss one! It took a piece of her face.
- Brad: I got it. The Bird is in charge, at least with me.
- Falconer: But the real answer to your question about trusting people to handle my Birds is quite simple. My Birds decide.
- Brad: How do the Birds decide?
- Falconer: If one of my Birds will not go on a person's arm, there is something very wrong about that person. Something the Bird sees or feels or understands that we cannot. So, you see, in the end, my Birds decide.
- Brad: If we used your Birds in organizations to interview and screen people we would save money on Human Resources. And how about at the airports instead of all those TSA teams. And maybe even in politics before we vote for people!
- Falconer: OK, let's focus on the woods ahead for now. My Birds don't like a lot of talking. Flying, hunting and eating, they like. They get bored with too much talking.
- Brad: Got it. (But I'm quietly thinking we have something here. Maybe in our follow-up book to The Business Zoo!)

Keys to the Zoo or What should you do next?

Ethics: develop a personal Moral code you are comfortable with:
- Be consistent in who you are, not what others say you are
- Know that grease and conflicts of interest are everywhere
- Avoid personal and management fraud as it ruins lives
- Try to use one code for business and life; it's easier

Career: to advance in your chosen field, keep open to:
- Different types of business-small/private or large/public
- Different activities like selling, systems or HR and how they should all work together
- Acquire an international frame of mind
- Use lunches and dinners to enhance work and life

Crisis: become both a planner and a crisis manager since:
- Planning can help in your personal and business life
- A crisis can occur anytime and for many reasons
- The worst is a leadership crisis
- The most lethal is a confidence crisis, so stay focused

Culture: become a lifelong student of organizations' cultures:

- Study your past leaders and critical events
- Understand how it affects systems, policies and rewards
- Help culture drive your firm to greatness
- Avoiding rigidity that cannot adapt or change
- Strive for continuity, transition and novelty
- Know that small and large firms can learn from each other

Leadership: Strive to become a true Leader by:

- Performing your own people duties, don't defer to others
- Studying what really motivates people and being creative
- Managing the many Wizards you will encounter
- Planning before you do deals and performing due diligence
- View your Board as an asset but make sure it's accountable

In Conclusion:

- Judge your own journey by how it ends not how it begins
- On your path, you never know what animals you'll meet
- Never show fear, it's deadly in a career or a zoo!

Thanks for sharing the journey! Brad.

www.ingramcontent.com/pod-product-compliance
Lightning Source LLC
Chambersburg PA
CBHW070809220326
41520CB00055B/6786